Basketball
SKILLS & DRILLS

Jerry V. Krause, EdD
Eastern Washington University

Leisure Press
Champaign, Illinois

Library of Congress Cataloging-in-Publication Data

Krause, Jerry.
  Basketball skills & drills / Jerry V. Krause.
    p.   cm.
  ISBN 0-88011-422-3
  1. Basketball--Coaching. I. Title. II. Title: Basketball skills
and drills.
GV885.3.K68 1991
796.323'077--dc20   90-24891
                                              CIP

ISBN: 0-88011-422-3

Developmental Editor: June I. Decker, PhD
Managing Editor: Robert King
Assistant Editors: Julia Anderson, Dawn Levy, and Valerie Hall
Copyeditor: Sam Cogdell
Proofreader: Terry Olive
Indexer: Barbara Cohen
Production Director: Ernie Noa
Typsetter: Yvonne Winsor
Text Design: Keith Blomberg
Text Layout: Denise Peters
Cover Design: Jack Davis
Cover Photo: Will Zehr
Interior art: Keith Blomberg, David Gregory, and Gretchen Walters
Printer: Versa Press

Leisure Press books are available at special discounts for bulk purchase for sales promotions, premiums, fundraising, or educational use. Special editions or book excerpts can also be created to specification. For details, contact the Special Sales Manager at Leisure Press.

Printed in the United States of America

10 9 8 7 6 5 4 3 2

Leisure Press
A Division of Human Kinetics Publishers, Inc.
Box 5076, Champaign, IL 61825-5076
1-800-747-4457

Canada Office:
Human Kinetics Publishers, Inc.
P.O. Box 2503, Windsor, ON N8Y 4S2
1-800-465-7301 (in Canada only)

UK Office:
Human Kinetics Publishers (UK) Ltd.
P.O. Box 18
Rawdon, Leeds LS19 6TG
England
(0532) 504211

Contents

Preface

Saying that basic skills are only for beginners is like saying that shacks need better foundations than skyscrapers. In fact the reverse is true. The higher a player or coach hopes to rise in basketball, the better his or her basic skills must be. Just as an error in stationary posture is amplified in movement, so too an error or weakness in a basic skill will disrupt performance of every higher-level skill.

In *Basketball Skills & Drills* I have provided thorough explanations of every skill, beginning with basic locomotor movements and leading to the fundamentals of offensive and defensive team play. Read the in-depth description of the skills, study the detailed drawings and diagrams, practice with the drills at the end of each chapter, and perfect and streamline your game from the bottom up. The explanations are comprehensive yet simple to understand, and the illustrations make the skills apparent at a glance.

Part I of the book addresses the individual basketball skills needed to play the game while Part II builds on these fundamentals with basics of team play.

Basketball Skills & Drills distills over 30 years of basketball coaching (all age and skill levels and both genders) into concepts that are easy to understand, apply, and master. Thus, *Basketball Skills & Drills* can function as a textbook for coaching theory classes and teaching-basketball lab classes, a guide for coaches and instructors, or a handy reference on fundamentals for coaches, players, and players' parents alike.

Acknowledgments

My primary appreciation goes to the players—the young men and young women I have been privileged to work with and learn from. The opportunity to learn from those players has been the catalyst for developing this book. It is my hope that future players will benefit from it as much as I have from developing it.

To the outstanding assistant coaches who have been my foundation and support, I am especially indebted. Each has affected my approach to teaching the game and has contributed to the ideas presented here.

In addition to these people there are four I single out for their strong positive influences on my growth and development as a person and a coach.

To them I dedicate this book:

George Sage, the first head coach that I had the privilege to work with at the college level. He provided me with the opportunity and encouragement to become a college coach and physical educator. His example as a true professional, educator, and coach has been my continual model.

Jack Leighton, former chairman of physical education at Eastern Washington University and a man of high principle who has dedicated his life to the physical education profession. He hired me in my first college teaching and coaching position and gave me the responsibility and freedom to grow and to develop my ideas.

John R. Wooden, former basketball coach at UCLA. He is enshrined as a player and coach in the Naismith Basketball Hall of Fame. When I was a young coach searching for assistance, and Coach Wooden was at the pinnacle of his career, he was patient and understanding in providing personal time and help as well as a professional example through his coaching and teaching. I will always appreciate his accessibility.

Ralph Miller, with whom I had the privilege of coaching during the 1982-83 season. He is one of the all-time greats in basketball coaching. I have found him a master at simplifying the game of basketball and life. He is a consummate strategist as well as a fine teacher of fundamentals. I will long treasure his counsel and guidance.

A final debt of gratitude is owed to my primary source of inspiration—my wife, Christy, who has provided meaning and balance to my basketball world.

Part I

Coaching the Individual

Chapters 1 through 8 address the individual basketball skills needed for success in any system of play. Team patterns depend heavily on the sum of the individual skills each player brings to the team, as well as on the proper use of these skills at the right time.

Universally, basketball players spend most of their individual practice time developing the offensive skills that involve the ball—dribbling, passing, catching, shooting, and rebounding. Few coaches encourage players to work on individual defensive skills, or offensive skills without the ball. I recommend that you focus on a balanced approach to players' self-development, coaching athletes to devote time to all the skills of the game. As a coach, emphasize the individual defensive skills and offensive moves without the ball to balance the typical overemphasis of ball-related offensive skills. This will ensure balanced and complete development of *all* players.

Chapter 1

Fundamental Movements

One of your first and foremost tasks is to teach players how to move and control their bodies. Fundamental movements are sometimes called the *basics* of basketball; they are essential tools for each of your players to learn.

You will need to teach each player to move effectively (because the bottom line is getting the job done) and also efficiently (moving the best way). Teach players to conserve time and space and to reduce wasted motion so they can develop balance and quickness. In other words, your players should always move with a purpose.

Basketball is a game of quickness (hand and foot) and speed (overall body motion), used at the proper time. Your coaching should continually emphasize the principle of doing things right, doing things quickly, and then making the right move quickly at the right time.

The five fundamental positions and movements of basketball that you will teach are basic position, starts, steps, stops, and jumps.

BASIC POSITION (OR STANCE)

Your players need to learn to be ready to move at all times, developing the habit of a good basic basketball position to ready them for quick movements. Teaching basic position is a challenging task, and you will need to be patient with younger players, who may not have the strength and muscle endurance to stay in position very long.

Teach players the feeling of good position—being ready for anything, feeling quick. Maintaining basic position is hard work; players must become comfortable in an awkward, unnatural, monkeylike position. Remind them frequently to get in and stay in their stance. If you consistently emphasize basic position early, your athletes will soon learn to assume it automatically.

Foot Position

The best foot placement in most situations is the staggered stance. Feet should be about shoulder-width apart, with the heel of one foot along the same horizontal line as the toes of the other (see Figure 1.1). This position should be used when a player needs to be able to move in any direction.

The parallel stance shown in Figure 1.2 is used for side-to-side movement, as well as for catching the ball and stopping, stopping after dribbling, and responding when a defender moves laterally. In time, players will learn which situations warrant which stance.

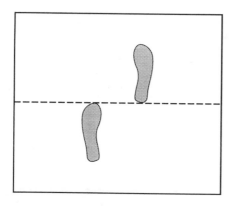

Figure 1.1 The staggered stance (top view). A heel-and-toe relationship, shoulder-width apart.

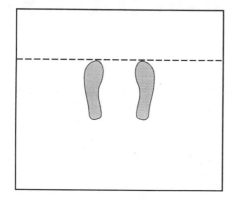

Figure 1.2 The parallel stance (top view). Toe-to-toe relationship, shoulder-width apart.

Weight Distribution

Body weight should be evenly distributed from side to side, from front to back, and between feet. Heels should be down, with most of the weight on the balls of the feet, although pressure should be felt on the toes and heels.

Players may incorrectly place all of their weight on the balls of the feet with the heels off the floor, but this position is slower—it requires that the heel be brought down before any forceful movement can take place. A good way to teach the feeling of proper position is to ask players to take an "eagle claw" position, with heels down and toes curled.

When players are on defense, they should add one more thing to their basic position—footfire. This means keeping the feet active and in constant motion without leaving the floor surface, a technique that helps keep leg muscles ready for action. Have players imagine that they are standing on a bed of hot coals, but don't let their feet leave the floor.

Head and Trunk Position

The head is a key to balance because of its relative size and location at the top of the body. Have players keep the head centered over the support base—the head should be the apex of a triangle, with the legs as two equal sides and a line between the feet as the base when seen from the front (Figure 1.3). The head is also to be centered from front to back. Players should be taught an erect trunk position with shoulders back and trunk slightly forward of vertical.

Figure 1.3 Head, the key to balance, carried up and alert—the apex of the triangle.

Arms and Legs

Teach players to keep their joints (ankles, knees, hips, shoulders, elbows, and wrists) bent and ready. The hands and arms should be bent and kept close to the body for balance and quickness. Remember, the whole foot bottom should be touching the floor. Remind the players to "stay low"—the angle at the knee joint in back of the legs should be 90 degrees to 120 degrees to maintain a low center of gravity.

COACHING POINTS FOR BASIC POSITION

- Be ready for action.
- Keep knees bent with hands and head up; get low.
- Stay in the stance.
- Keep weight on the whole foot with the heels down.

STARTS, STEPS, AND STOPS

Starting, stepping (pivots, moves, turns), and stopping are the fundamental movements used to move effectively and efficiently in and out of basic stance. These are called offensive and defensive "moves." Remember the coaching rule: teach players to first do it right (execute the skill correctly), then do it quickly, and finally, do it at the right time, every time.

A player's overall speed is important but not as critical as quickness (hand-foot speed). As a coach, you need to strive to improve the quickness of each player. Thinking quick and being quick should be your players' constant focus.

Starts

Starting is the first skill your players must learn that uses basic position. To start quickly players should shift their weight in the desired direction of movement. For example, to move to the left, body weight is shifted over the left foot by leaning to the left. Remind players that because the head is the key to balance it always leads the weight shift (Figure 1.4).

In order to be quick at the right time, players must remember that all motion change begins on the floor. This means taking short, choppy steps whenever a change of motion is needed. Teach players to keep their feet in contact with the floor as much as possible; teach them that they can use the floor to their advantage by staying close to it.

Figure 1.4 Moving laterally left: weight to the desired direction of movement (over left foot).

Front Foot First

From basic position, players should shift weight in the direction of movement and start by taking the first step with the nearest foot. For example, to move to the right, the first step is taken with the right foot; to move forward, the first step is with the front foot.

Point-Push-Pull

On defense, players should use a sliding motion. Have them keep feet at shoulder width and use very short, quick shuffle steps. This technique is called point-push-pull. The lead foot points in the direction of desired movement as a short, quick slide step (lead foot first) is taken (Figure 1.5). The force for the point and slide step comes from a push from the trail foot, which moves the body and transfers the weight to the lead foot. This is

Figure 1.5 Point and push.

quickly followed by a pulling slide step taken with the trail foot to regain basic position.

Players should learn to execute defensive starts and slides in side-to-side, forward, backward, and diagonal directions, all done with the head level. Watch for head-bouncing that shows that a player is bouncing along instead of sliding and is not staying in a stance. Such bouncing, known as the "bunny hop," means losing the floor as a friend and is a waste of time and space. Emphasize to players that the head must be kept level.

COACHING POINTS FOR STARTS

- Be ready to start by maintaining basic stance.
- Learn that using the floor works to your advantage; keep feet on the floor when starting.
- Shift your weight in the desired direction of movement, and lead with the head moving first in that direction.
- Stay down and pump the arms when starting.
- Use the principle of front or lead foot first.
- For defensive slides, use the point-push-pull technique.
- Move and start in straight lines.

Steps (Pivots)

Turning, or pivoting, is motion that rotates the body in a circular fashion around the ball of one foot while the player maintains basic position (Figure 1.6).

As the basic skill for beginning all motion changes, the pivot is one of the most important player tools for quickness and balance. It is also one of the least used and poorly learned skills in basketball.

Pivoting can be done upon either foot as the stationary center of rotation. When body rotation is toward the front—a pivoting motion that moves the trunk forward around the pivot—the pivot is called a front turn (see Figure 1.7). Likewise, a rear turn is used to pivot a player's backside to the rear (Figure 1.8).

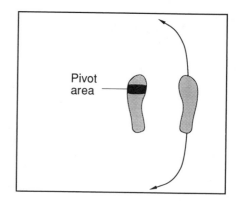

Figure 1.6 Pivoting: a rotation of the body where the ball of the nonpivoting foot remains stationary.

Figure 1.7 Right foot pivot—front turn. Starting position (a) and ending position (b).

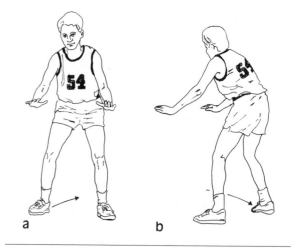

Figure 1.8 Left-foot pivot—rear turn. Starting position (a) and ending position (b).

Players must learn to make pivots with and without the ball on offense. On defense, the pivot is the first move that players use when changing from one position to another and

Figure 1.9 Changing position (a) and rebounding (b).

COACHING POINTS FOR PIVOTS

- Stay down in basic stance and keep the head level.
- Keep the feet wide apart.
- Maintain balance and keep the head up.
- Pivot quickly but properly.
- Use the pivot to turn up to a half turn (180 degrees); repeat pivots if more turning is necessary.

---

when rebounding, as illustrated in Figure 1.9.

Stops

Being quick with balance and control means that players must be able to use basic position, start properly, move quickly (by running or sliding), and finally stop quickly in a balanced position.

The two recommended basic basketball stops are the one-count "quick stop" and the two-count "stride stop."

Quick Stop

The preferred stop for beginners is the quick stop, sometimes called the jump stop. The quick stop is executed at the end of a running or sliding motion. When running, a player does a quick stop by jumping slightly from one foot, skimming the floor surface, and landing in a parallel or staggered stance (basic position—see Figure 1.10). Both feet hit the floor at the same time (one count).

The quick stop is almost always useful because it conserves time and space—it takes only one count and occurs quickly, it can be used on defense or offense (with or without the ball), and it is a complement to the pivot, one of the primary tools of body control and movement. Basketball rules allow players to use either foot for pivoting after a quick stop. This gives them a wide variety of motion

Figure 1.10 Quick stop (a) and landing in basic position (b).

**COACHING POINTS
FOR STOPS**

- Use the quick stop unless changing direction (180 degrees) when running; then use the stride stop.
- When using the quick stop, jump from one foot and land in basic position on two feet at once. Stay close to the floor.
- Stay low and sit on the back foot when making the stride stop.

---

possibilities with control and balance. The quick stop is important for getting into quick basic position for shooting, passing, or dribbling and can be used very effectively after dribbling or receiving a pass.

Stride Stop

The stride stop is a two-count stop executed by landing on the rear foot (first count) with the front foot hitting immediately afterward (second count). Its primary use is to reverse direction when running forward. For all other motion situations, players should use the quick stop.

JUMPS

Jumping is an especially important skill in a sport with an elevated goal. Coaches often consider jumping a natural ability that players have or do not have and a skill that cannot be taught. Nothing could be further from the truth.

There are basic principles for improving jumping skill. First, players need to be taught to be in basic stance ready to jump. When players learn to be ready to jump, then it is possible for them to jump quickly in any situation.

Second, your players will be able to jump higher if they increase the muscle strength in their legs. Coaches should help players improve their leg strength through resistance training as well as their jumping skill.

Third, it should be pointed out to players that how they land after a jump will determine how quickly and how high their next immediate jump will be. The best landing position is in basic stance with balance and a wide base. A player is then ready to jump again. Body position and control are best taught when players have first learned to jump using both feet and both arms.

The sections that follow explain how to execute two-foot jumps, one-foot jumps, and quick jumps and when to use each one in game situations.

Two-Foot Jumps

A two-foot takeoff for jumping is slower than jumping from one foot on the move. It is best used when players are in high-traffic situations (such as battling a crowd of players for a rebound) or on power lay-ups with close defenders.

The takeoff foot (or feet) should be planted firmly before the jump is made (players should visualize themselves stamping their feet through the floor) to provide maximum leg-muscle contraction.

Teach players to use momentum transfer whenever possible, by (a) using the forward momentum of a running jump with forceful contact on the takeoff foot (or feet), and (b) swinging the arms forcefully to add to the body's momentum (when time and space permit) (Figure 1.11).

One-Foot Jumps

Jumping from one foot is benefical when movement and maximum height are required. Players should know how to do one-foot takeoffs so they can attack the basket on lay-ups and jump high toward the basket or backboard.

Quick Jumps

Quick jumps are the best compromise between conserving time and space and maintaining body position and control. A quick jump should be used wherever there is congestion, contact, or a contested jump around the basketball. These are two-foot–two-hand

a   b

Figure 1.11 Ready position (a) and quick jump (b).

jumps without momentum that start from basic position. The hands are held head high with the upper arms near horizontal before a quick jump is made.

COACHING POINTS FOR JUMPS

- Be ready to jump—Get in basic position, jump, and land in basic position.
- Jump from two feet with two hands most of the time (especially when rebounding).
- Use a two-foot takeoff for power and control and a one-foot takeoff for speed and height.
- Use momentum transfer from running forward and from the arms swinging upward whenever there is time.
- Use quick jumps whenever possible.
- Use quick stops and quick jumps when shooting a jump shot.

FUNDAMENTAL MOVEMENT DRILLS

STANCE CHECK

Purpose: To develop the skill of recognizing various basic stances, getting in a basic stance, and maintaining that stance.

Equipment: Half-court floor space (minimum).

Procedure: Players spread out on the basketball court facing the coach, assume a basic stance variation as directed, and maintain the stance while it is checked by a coach (or partner).

STANCE MIRROR

Purpose: To self-evaluate stance variations by recognizing the "look" of a good stance.

Equipment: Player and full-length mirror.

Procedure: Each player checks all stance variations in front of a mirror, holding each basic stance at least 5 seconds. A partner system may also be used if a mirror is not available.

LINE STARTS, STEPS, STOPS

Purpose: To develop skill in starting, pivoting, and stopping.

Equipment: Full court.

Procedure: All players are divided into four groups behind the baseline at one end of the court with the coach in the middle (Figure 1.12). The coach calls out the option players are to perform.

Options:

- Stutter-steps—Start from baseline and go to the opposite end line, keeping the hands up, and making the shoes squeak. Remember to use the floor to your advantage.
- Change-of-pace moves—Alternate two or three slow and fast moves after a quick start. Be quick and use a varied number of steps (avoid the same patterns).

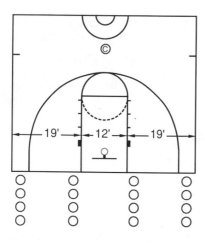

Figure 1.12 Line starts, steps, and stops.

- Pivots—Full front and rear turns (the same as stride stop variation).
- Split-vision jog—Four players start simultaneously and jog at half speed focusing on the far basket while using their peripheral vision to stay in a straight line from side to side.
- Quick stops—At free throw line, half-court line, and opposite free throw line.

Note: Coaches may hold players in any quick stop position to check their position and correct mistakes. Players may imagine they are dribbling a ball or sprinting without the ball (on offense). If defensive quick stops are used, the feet should be active at all times.

- Stride stops—Progressive forward and backward moves are made from the baseline to the free throw line (stride stop, reverse), back to the baseline (reverse), from the baseline to the half-court line (reverse), back to the free throw line, and then to the opposite free throw line, back to the half-court line, and then to the opposite baseline, and so on (Figure 1.13).
- Spacing jog (a more advanced skill that can also be used with change-of-pace moves)—The first four players start on command and move at their own paces. The next person in line starts when the player ahead is 15 to 18 feet away and maintains that distance. This is especially challenging in combination with change-of-pace moves.

Note: The coach can advance to a "whistle stop" drill; four players start and on each short whistle they stride-stop (or quick-stop), then reverse and sprint until the next whistle. The next group of four players always starts on the second whistle after the previous group. The drill continues until a player reaches the opposite baseline and all players have run the floor. This is an excellent conditioning drill.

Drill Reminders

- Each variation is done in one circuit (down and back).
- The first players in each line should always come to basic position on the

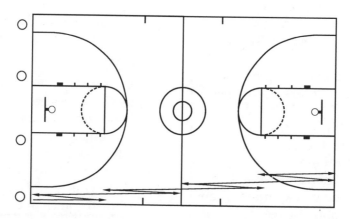

Figure 1.13 Stride stops option.

baseline and be ready before being required to move. Players should listen for the direction and command ''go'' from coaches.

- Equal side-to-side floor spacing should be kept when initiating movement.
- Unless directed otherwise, subsequent groups of four begin moving when the previous group reaches the near free throw line.
- All groups move to the opposite baseline and re-form with the first group of four in basic position ready to come back in the opposite direction.

LINE QUICK JUMPS

Purpose: To develop basic jumping skills for rebounding and shooting.

Equipment: Half-court floor space (minimum).

Procedure: Players are in four lines on the baseline with coach near half-court line. One ''down and back'' circuit of quick jumps can be added. The first wave of players sprints forward from basic position on the command ''go.'' Every time a ''thumbs-up'' signal is given, players execute a quick stop into a quick jump. They continue to repeat quick jumps in place until the coach signals them to run forward again with a ''hitchhiking'' sign. The first group sprints again as the next group starts from basic position on the end line. This is repeated until all groups reach the opposite end line. The coach must be in front of and visible to all groups so the players can see his or her signals.

JUMP BALL TIPPING

Purpose: To develop jumping skills for jump ball situations.

Equipment: A ball for each jump circle, players in pairs, jump circles.

Procedure: Using basic jumping techniques, practice in pairs at the three jump circles having a player or coach toss the ball in the air for the jump ball situation.

Chapter 2

Moves Without the Ball

One of the most difficult coaching tasks is to teach your players to carry out actions that don't involve the basketball—the magnet of our game. An individual player (with five players on a team) will be playing without the basketball over 80% of the time while on offense.

This figure illustrates the considerable importance of developing individual skills that do not involve possession of the basketball. Many coaches believe that this is a problem area with most young players. These players are often "magnetized" by the ball and seem to be almost obsessively attracted to the ball on offense. Considerable time must be spent teaching them that movement without the ball can be just as important in setting up scoring opportunities as moves made with the ball. Helping players understand this is the key to motivating them to carry out purposeful movement when they do not have the ball.

FUNDAMENTALS OF MOVING WITHOUT THE BALL

In order for players to move effectively without the ball, there are certain fundamentals they must master and remember on the court.

- Be alert and remember that all moves begin *on the floor*.
- Move with authority, balance, and quickness.
- Move with a purpose—Players must be aware of teammates' movement and maintain their focus on the offensive strategies of the whole team.
- Read the defense and the ball—All individual movement is dictated by the team play situation, but it must be carried out with relation to the position and movement of the ball as well as the opponents' defense. Players must be taught to get open by moving to clear areas on the court where they can receive passes.
- Get open or get out—The primary purpose of movement without the ball is to get open to receive a pass from the ballhandler. Players should learn to first try to get open and then, if this is not possible, to get out of the way.
- Use the perfect catching position—This is a position 15 to 20 feet from the ballhandler where players are open to receive the ball. Ideally, this will also be in a floor position affording the players the option to pass, shoot, or dribble.
- Be an actor—Movement without the ball is a continuous competition between the offensive and defensive players; keeping

opponents guessing requires using believable fakes to bait the defenders and playing the role of decoy.

- Lose the defender—Move out of the defenders' fields of vision and force them to turn their heads. Since most defenders have their backs to the basket and their eyes on the ball, offensive players should move behind them to the baseline and away from the ball. Cuts can best be made from this position because it is difficult for defenders to anticipate moves.

- Run through leather—When moving to catch a pass it is important for players to maintain the "open position" by moving toward and meeting the pass, unless they're making a breakaway move to the basket ahead of the defender.

- Get close to get open—Because this rule goes against common sense, many players make the mistake of trying to free themselves by staying away from a defender. It is actually more effective to stay close to the defender and then break away quickly to get open. This move is almost always effective because it allows the offensive player to execute an action move that is made before and is quicker than the defender's reaction move.

BASIC MOVES (WITHOUT BALL)

Basic moves without the ball should be taught to every player. Most of these moves require that the player be deceptive in order to fool the defense.

V-Cuts

Special-purpose cuts or moves will also include "fake-and-break," or V-cuts (basic zig-zag or change-of-direction cuts that form the shape of a V). To execute a V-cut, place weight on foot opposite desired direction, point lead foot, and step with this opposite foot. For example, push from right foot and step to the left with the left foot. One side of the V is usually the move to the basket, away from the basket, or to the defender. The other

side of the V is the quick change-of-direction cut to get open (see Figure 2.1). Young players can best be taught this by using the term fake-and-break for the V-cut to get open. The first part of the V-move to the basket or the defender (the fake) is done slowly and is quickly followed by the last part of the V (the break) to get open. The break move is usually toward the ball.

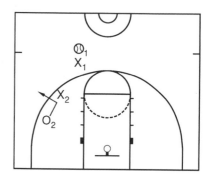

Figure 2.1   Get close to get open. O_2 moves close to X_2 then makes a quick V-cut move to get open to receive a pass.

Front and Rear Cuts

These are moves made after a player has passed the ball to a teammate and wants to challenge the defense by cutting to the basket for a possible return pass. The pass-and-cut move—sometimes called "give-and-go" basketball—is one of the most valuable offensive moves in the game.

The give and go takes two forms: the preferred front cut, which allows the offensive player to receive the ball in front of the defender (an excellent scoring position), and the rear cut, which lets the offensive player cut behind the defender to gain an advantage going to the basket (Figure 2.2). Note that a front cut uses a V-cut to set up the defense whereas the rear cut is a direct, straight-line cut.

Decoy Moves

Decoy moves are any of the basic moves used to keep defenders busy, such as distracting defensive players from helping defend against a ballhandler or trap the ball. Teach

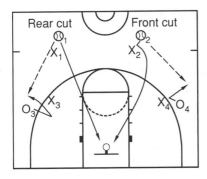

Figure 2.2 Front and rear cuts—give-and-go basketball.

players to be actors and distractors: misleading defenders with deceptive eye movements, physical bluffs, and other visual or auditory distractions.

Shot Moves

When the ball is in the air on a shot attempt by the offensive team, each offensive player should either move to a rebounding position or go to a defensive assignment depending upon their position. Players should be taught to never be caught standing still watching the ball.

Assigned Moves

Assigned moves are individually assigned cuts in a system of play for special situations. Coaches make these specific assignments for jump balls, out-of-bounds plays, free throws, and set patterns. All players must carry out individual assignments properly and quickly. How well this is done is just as important as what is being done.

Screen Moves

Setting and using screens to get a teammate open for a pass or a drive is one of the most unselfish team moves players can learn. This also includes being able to use screens as an essential skill of individual offense. Instruction in setting and using screens should begin at the secondary level—elementary school players should concentrate on learning the other moves without the ball.

Types of Screens

Screens can be classified according to location (on the ball or away from the ball), how they are used (up screens that are set behind or on the blind side of a defender, down screens that are set in front of or to the side of a defender), and by the kind of body contact used to screen (front or rear of body).

Coaches should develop their own theories of how screens should work. Some coaches advocate screening a certain spot or area on the floor (position screen), whereas others believe in screening the defender (player screen). A player screen is usually more effective in freeing the offensive player but may result in more fouls being charged for illegal screens, or blocks. - CHARGING, ACTUALLY -

Setting Screens

Setting a screen is a basic move that should be taught as follows. Players should use a noisy, quick stop with the feet shoulder-width apart and the hands out of the screen (Figure 2.3). The screen should be set perpendicular to the expected path of the defender and should be forceful enough for the defender to see and hear it. Screening players should be loud, low, wide, and ready for contact. Against good defensive teams, the cutter will usually be covered, but the screener will often be open.

Figure 2.3 Front screen: noisy quick stop with wide base, keeping arms out of screen. Here screener is on right.

Other tips on screening include using down screens (toward the basket) against "sagging" defenders and up screens (away from the basket) against pressure or "overplaying" defenders.

Using Screens

The most difficult screening skill is to prepare the defender to run into the screen (players should use a teammate as an obstacle) with a V-cut, usually started toward the basket as shown in Figure 2.4.

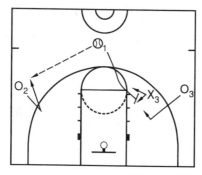

Figure 2.4 Using the screen, O_3 is setting up the defender (X_3) to run into the screener (O_1) by using a V-cut.

Players should cut "razor close" to the screener so that they are shoulder to shoulder. On screens away from the ball, players using a screen should be in basic position as they pass the screen with hands up, ready to receive a pass. Timing is a crucial factor in effective screen plays: Players must wait for the screen to be set before making their moves.

Movement Mistakes

Movement mistakes occur when a player without the ball commits an error. Teach players to focus their attention on recovery, call out for help from teammates when needed, and get in position for the next play immediately. This is especially important when an offensive error results in an interception.

COACHING POINTS FOR MOVING WITHOUT THE BALL

- Use the floor to advantage when beginning a move.
- Move with authority.
- Move with a purpose.
- Read the defense and the ball, then react.
- Get open or get out of the way—Don't stand still.
- Know and use the perfect catching position.
- Be an actor—Take the initiative, use believable fakes, seem to aggressively pursue the ball.
- Lose the defender.
- Run through leather.
- Get close to get open.
- Set strong, noisy, and legal screens.
- Set picks or screens at right angles to the expected path of the defender.

DRILLS FOR MOVING WITHOUT THE BALL

LINE MOVES WITHOUT THE BALL

Purpose: To teach basic moves without the ball by simulation.

Equipment: Half court (minimum).

Procedure: The players should assume a basic four-line drill position on the baseline. The first player in each line moves from side to side without the ball, imagining the ball to be in the center of the court (Figure 2.5).

Options:

- V-cuts to get open (designated to the basket and to the ball or to the defender and to the ball)—Repeated V-cuts followed by quick stops to simulate catching the ball the length of the court.
- V-cut to get open followed by a backdoor cut. Proper footwork and hand position

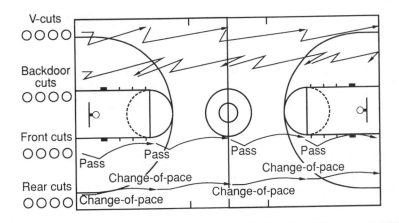

Figure 2.5 Line drill: V-cuts, backdoor cuts, front cuts, and rear cuts without the ball.

are emphasized (keep hands up—get open; outside hand down—backdoor).

- Front cuts—A simulated pass to the center of the court is followed by a front cut (V-cut, slow move away, fast cut to the ball) and quick stop at the free throw lines and the half-court line.
- Rear cuts—A simulated pass to the center of the court is followed by a rear cut (change-of-pace; slow to fast) and quick stop at the free throw lines and the half-court line.

Note: Quick stops are used at each free throw line and the half-court line. At the completion of each quick stop, players

should challenge the imaginary defense by using a "catch-and-face" move: first quick stop, then pivot and face the basket, looking over the whole court.

V-CUT

Purpose: To teach players the basic moves without the ball in a two-on-zero, two-on-two situation.

Equipment: One ball per basket per group.

Procedure: The basic two-line formation for this drill is one line of guards or point position players out front and a line of forwards or wing position players on the side.

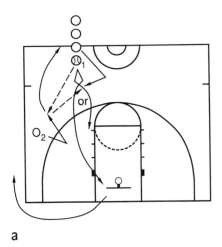

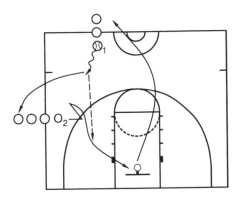

a   b

Figure 2.6 V-cut drill (a) and backdoor (b).

Options:

- Forwards V-cut to get open (fake and break) and after receiving the pass from the guard, catch and face the basket (Figure 2.6a).
- Guard makes front or rear cut to basket and goes to the end of the forward line V (give and go) (Figure 2.6a).
- Forward then passes to next guard in line and goes to the end of the guard line.
- Figure 2.6b shows a forward ''backdoor'' move performed during a guard dribble move.

Note: The forward V-cut may be a fake to the basket and break to get open or to the imaginary defender.

- When acceptable skill levels are reached, add two defenders and execute the drills in a two-on-two situation.

Chapter 3

Ballhandling

Ballhandling encompasses all offensive moves with the basketball—passing, catching, dribbling, shooting, individual moves, and rebounding. For our purposes, this chapter's discussion of ballhandling includes only the skills of passing, catching, and dribbling.

The arm mechanics of the ballhandling skills of passing, dribbling, and shooting are almost identical—the arm and hand motion is the same for each skill. Passing and catching are the most important of all the individual offensive fundamentals with the ball; shooting will be considered as a pass to the basket. Dribbling is a secondary offensive weapon that should never be misused or overused.

Getting into triple-threat position, where a player with the ball may shoot, pass, or dribble, should become an automatic action. The underlying concept is that players, when they become ballhandlers, should first look to pass the ball to a teammate (unless open themselves for a scoring opportunity within range) before choosing to dribble—the final option for moving the ball.

PASSING AND CATCHING

Passing and catching are the most neglected fundamentals in basketball. It is essential that players develop these skills in order to mount a successful team offense. Effective passing and receiving in the form of the scoring assist is a measure of the degree of offensive teamwork, and can also be an important tool for controlling game tempo on offense.

Insure that players who are good passers and receivers have an excellent chance to be important team members. From a coaching standpoint, good passing tends to take the pressure off a team's defensive play and to break down the opponent's defense. Because passing is the quickest way to move the ball and challenge the defense, it should be the primary weapon of your team's offensive attack. Develop the notion that passing and catching are the best offensive team plays by explaining that they are the most effective way of achieving the offensive objective—getting the ball to an open player to set up a scoring opportunity.

Passing Principles

There are a number of fundamental elements of passing that should be taught. Good passes can only be made when these factors are present:

- Quickness—The ball must be passed quickly (before the defender has time to react). The pass should be snappy and crisp, but not too hard or too easy.

- A target—Each pass must be accurately thrown to a specific target (usually away from the defender).
- Timing—The ball must be delivered when the receiver is open and not before or after.
- Trickery—The passer must use deception to confuse the defender, who is reading the passer (especially the eyes) and anticipating the pass.

Passers should visually locate all teammates on the court as well as defenders, concentrating on the potential receiver without staring. This can best be done by surveying the whole floor area with the ball in triple-threat position. When they catch a pass, players should always be prepared to shoot when open and within range; if unable to shoot themselves, they should then try to pass to an open teammate before resorting to dribbling to move the ball.

Players must learn to unselfishly give up the ball by passing to an open player. Ball-handlers can also penetrate and pass—they can create an opportunity for an assist by making a dribble move that allows them to pass to a teammate open to score.

When players are passing the choice should be to make the easy pass through or by the defender. Teach players not to gamble on passes. They should be clever, not fancy.

Choosing the Correct Pass

The quickest passes are air passes. Simple geometry (the shortest distance between two points is a straight line) proves that the air pass is quicker than either the lob pass or the bounce pass, as shown in Figure 3.1. There-

fore, the air pass is the primary pass to use. All perimeter passes around the defense should be air passes.

Lob passes are used only when passing to

- teammates on a breakaway fast break when the lob allows them to run to catch up with the ball, and
- teammates being fronted while playing a low post position.

Bounce passes are used only when passing to

- players in the post position who are smaller than the defender,
- post players open on the baseline side,
- players making a backdoor cut, or
- players in an emergency.

Special Passing Situations

Other aspects related to passing must also be covered. These include movement by the passer after a pass is made and the dangers of passing into corners, along sidelines, or near out-of-bounds lines. Players should be taught never to pass across under the defensive basket—an interception there usually results in a score by the opponents. When a pass comes back out on the perimeter from the baseline, players should reverse the ball quickly to the other side of the court to test the defense and check for opponents' alertness.

Types of Passes

There are several types of passes used in basketball. The one used must fit a particular situation.

Chest Pass

The chest pass is the basic air pass for effective, efficient ball movement. The starting position for the pass is reached by moving the ball from triple-threat position to the center of the chest close to the body in a "thumbs-up" position. To throw the pass, a player then extends the elbows and pronates the

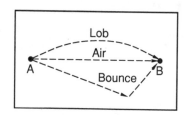

Figure 3.1 Types of passes—their path and distance traveled.

arms (rotates outward) to a "thumbs-down" ending position. Remind players to push the thumbs through the ball to produce a backspin on the ball. Players should take a step forward to pass when there is time, but passing without stepping is quicker. The target of the pass is the receiver's throat (neck) area when he or she is stationary and toward the receiver's outside hand or shoulder when he or she is moving near a defender.

Bounce Pass

This pass is recommended primarily for backdoor moves and emergencies when the passer must get out of a trap or when the defender is playing in high-passing lanes. Passing tips include making the pass to a target two-thirds of the way to the receiver, following through to that spot on the floor. The technique used is the same as for a chest pass. The pass should be thrown hard enough that it bounces up to the receiver at hip level. Starting with the ball in a thumbs-up position, passers should then push the thumbs through the ball and follow through to a thumbs-down position. The backspin this movement produces increases the angle of rebound on the bounce pass, making it easier to handle (Figure 3.2). Players may also step forward with the pass when there is time.

Overhead Pass

This is a valuable pass over the defense; it is especially effective against zone defenses. The position of the ball allows the passer to show the ball and use pass fakes. Teach players to keep the ball up—they should start with and keep elbows extended. The pass is thrown with the wrists and fingers—the ball should be overhead with no windup behind the head.

The technique involves starting with thumbs back, then pushing thumbs through the ball, and finishing with thumbs forward (Figure 3.3). The target is at the receiver's head level since this pass has a tendency to drop. The ball should be kept up by throwing to a high target; the pass is hard to handle when it is dropping. For more power, players should step forward with the pass.

Baseball Pass

A baseball pass is used to throw the long pass (usually over half-court length). The essential teaching points are as follows: Players should keep two hands on the ball as long as possible. They should use a stance with the body parallel to the sidelines and then plant the back foot, step with the front foot, and throw the ball by the ear, similar to a baseball catcher's throw. Proper follow-through includes carrying out a full pronation and extension of

a   b

Figure 3.2 Bounce pass: thumbs-up starting position (target is spot on the floor; a) and thumbs-down ending position (follow through to the spot; b).

a   b

Figure 3.3 Overhead pass: thumbs-back starting position (ball up, elbows locked; a) and thumbs forward (use wrist and fingers, keep ball up; b).

the arm ending with the thumb down (Figure 3.4). Players should only throw this pass with the dominant arm, using the off hand to fake the pass.

Push Pass

This is a quick pass used to pass through or by a closely guarding defender. It may be an air or bounce pass and should be used from the triple-threat position; the key is the bent-

elbow starting position. The passer should work one side of the defender's body, especially past the ear, where the biggest gap usually appears. The pass is made above or below the defender's arms after finding an opening through which to pass. Vertical fakes are used as players "read" the defense (Figure 3.5).

Catching Principles

Catching the basketball requires a player to be ready—potential pass receivers should be in basic position with both hands up. They must be open and giving a target at the right time.

"Run through leather" is another receiving rule that means to meet the pass unless the player is cutting to the basket on a backdoor cut or a breakaway situation. When defended, the receiver must move toward the ball until contact is made to ensure possession.

Players should catch the ball in the air whenever possible. The receiver should catch the ball with both feet in the air and come to a quick stop. This ensures body control, ball possession, and a quick return to basic position.

Playing two-handed basketball is a good habit to develop in your players. They should always catch the ball with both hands. There

a   b   c

Figure 3.4 Baseball pass: starting position—by the ear, both hands on the ball (a); pull the string—the fake pass can be used from this position (b); and pronate (thumbs down) on release (c).

Figure 3.5 Push pass: triple-threat position (a); work one side of the defender's body, the hole by the ear (b); and use vertical fakes (c).

are three methods of catching the ball. The first is with two hands up (thumbs together), used when the pass is near the middle of the body and above the waist (Figure 3.6). The second is with two hands down (thumbs apart), used when the pass is near the middle of the body and below the waist (Figure 3.7). The third method is the block and tuck, used when the pass is to either side of the body. The ball is blocked with one hand and tucked with the other hand. Both hands should be placed on the ball immediately (Figure 3.8).

The receiver should let the wrist and elbows give as the pass is caught. This is sometimes called developing "soft hands."

Figure 3.7 Two hands down catch for passes below the waist.

Figure 3.6 Two hands up catch for passes above waist.

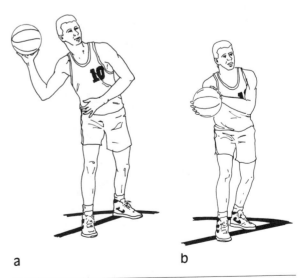

Figure 3.8 Block (a) and tuck (b) for passes to the side.

Another tip: The eyes should be focused on the pass until it is in both hands. Tell players to "catch the ball with their eyes" by looking the ball into their hands.

COACHING POINTS FOR PASSING AND CATCHING

- Teach triple-threat position.
- Help passers develop quickness, sense of target, timing, and trickery.
- Teach players to pass and catch with two hands whenever possible.
- Teach players to catch the ball with their feet in the air and to watch the ball until it is in their hands.
- Players should learn to catch and immediately scan the whole court.
- Train receivers to be ready for bad passes.

DRIBBLING

Dribbling is a touch skill, not a sight skill. Players should learn to dribble up the court without watching the ball. This can be accomplished by focusing on the offensive basket while dribbling and looking over the whole court (using peripheral vision). The primary objective is to create a move that allows a player to pass to a teammate for a score. Situations calling for dribbling are the live ball move, a basket penetration move going by an opponent using the dribble to drive for the basket, and ball movement to get a teammate open. Dribbling is also an acceptable option for advancing the ball up the court when a pass is not available, maneuvering for better position for a pass to a teammate, executing an offensive play or pattern, and getting out of heavy defensive traffic or a trap situation.

Dribbling Technique

The dribble is executed by first extending the elbow and flexing the wrist and fingers. The ball is controlled by the fingers and pads of the hand (the ball should be kept off the heel of the hand); the fingers are spread comfortably and should be cupped around the ball (Figure 3.9). It is important to maintain maximum contact with the ball. The rules of basketball require that the hand stay on top of the ball; the dribble is legal as long as the hand does not leave its vertical position to get under and carry the ball. The ball must leave the dribbler's hand before the pivot foot leaves the floor when starting a dribble.

It is strongly recommended that the quick stop be used to terminate the dribble (Figure 3.10). This stop is commonly thought to be

a   b

Figure 3.9   Dribbling: use fingers and pads of hands (a), elbow flexion, and wrist-finger flexion to push (b).

Figure 3.10 Terminate the dribble with a quick stop.

Feet even

Jump-stop

purpose. This is a general dribbling rule. On drives to the basket, the dribbler goes past the defender; the objective is to use one dribble to score. Bouncing the ball once or dribbling while not changing floor position (called "dropping" the ball) should be discouraged. A dribble penetration is best accomplished just after receiving a pass; this avoids forcing the dribble.

Another key guideline is to stay away from trouble with the dribble. Players should avoid dribbling in traffic (between two defenders) and keep alert for traps by watching for the defenders and avoiding the corners of the court (Figure 3.12).

the best method of avoiding traveling violations while conserving critical time and space for passing or shooting.

Players should learn to use either hand to dribble. Help them develop the weak hand but use the preferred hand whenever possible. They should always use the hand away from the defender when closely guarded. Teach players to protect the ball with the body and the opposite hand when dribbling against a close defender. They should keep the ball low and to the side of the body, and stay in basic stance (Figure 3.11).

Dribbling Strategies

When the ball is put on the floor the dribbler should always be going somewhere with a

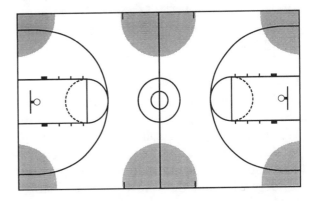

Figure 3.12 Stay out of trouble with the ball—avoid the corners of the basketball court.

Players should keep the dribble's momentum high and conclude a dribble with a pass or shot, preferably after a quick stop. A dribbler should use the right move at the right time and see the whole court ahead as well as teammates and defenders. *OH YEAH –*

Dribble Moves

The right type of dribble should be used at the right time. A low or control dribble should be used around defenders when the dribbler is closely guarded and a high or speed dribble should be used in the open court when advancing the ball.

Control Dribble

A control or low dribble is the first and easiest dribble to teach your players. They should

Figure 3.11 Closely guarded dribbler: protect the ball with the body and opposite hand, keep tension on legs, and stay in basic position.

use a staggered stance, in basic position with the ball-side foot back. The opposite hand is used for protection from the defender. It cannot be used to push the defender back or hook the defender, but only to protect the ball. The basic body motion is a sliding movement similar to defensive slides.

Players should protect the ball by dribbling on the side of the body away from the defensive player and keeping the ball low.

Speed Dribble

A speed or high dribble is taught next. Players should push the ball out in front and run after it, keeping it ahead of them. The ball can be dribbled higher—near waist level—to attain more speed. The faster the movement, the farther out front and the higher the ball should be pushed.

Change-of-Pace Dribble

A change-of-pace move is accomplished by changing speeds, in a stop-and-start motion. When slowing or stopping, dribblers should straighten up slightly to relax the defender. This move should be used to move past defenders who take the ''slow pace'' or ''stop'' fake. This is another slow-fast move to get dribblers in the clear and keep them open.

Head-and-Shoulders Move

A head-and-shoulders move is an advanced move. It is a dribble move to get around a defender using the preferred hand (Figure 3.13).

The ball is dribbled with the preferred hand. Then the move is continued by a fake opposite with a zigzag move on the opposite foot as a head-and-shoulders fake is made to that side. The ball is kept in rhythm with that move. The move past the defender is then made with the preferred foot. The rhythm is right/left/right to step by (when dribbling on the right side of the body). The advantage of this faking move is that the dribbler can face and see the defense while executing a dribble move to get around a defender with the preferred hand. The count for a right-handed person is (1) push from right foot as the dribble is made, (2) fake left with the foot, head, and shoulders, (3) extend the right foot with a long step as the ball is pushed out in front, and (4) step with the left foot and go to the basket.

Head-and-Shoulders Crossover

A head-and-shoulders crossover is another advanced move. It is a dribble move to cross the ball over from the preferred hand to the

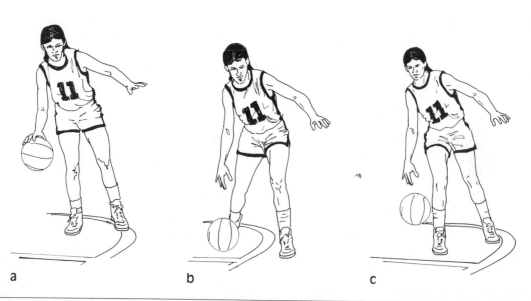

Figure 3.13 Head-and-shoulders move: weight on right foot, dribble ball on right side (a); zigzag on left foot, head-and-shoulders fake to left (b); and move past the defender with right foot (c).

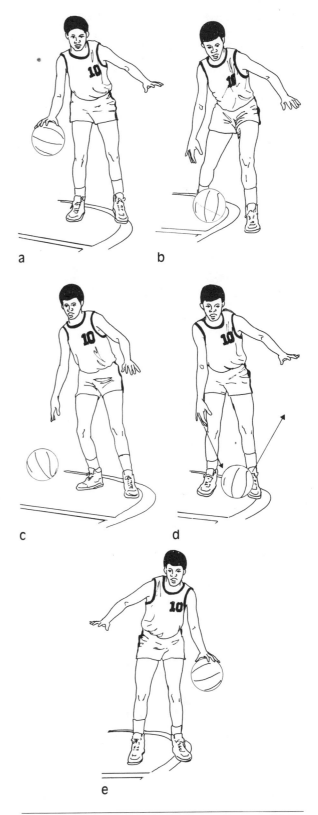

other hand while the dribbler moves past the defender on that side while still facing the defense (Figure 3.14). This move begins similarly to the head-and-shoulders move. The crossover dribble is kept low and is made across the body at the same time the zigzag move is made from the preferred side to the other side. The footwork is right/left/right/left to crossover from right to left and reverse when going from left to right. The dribble rhythm is timed with the footwork movement. The move must be made before the defender is close enough to reach the crossover dribble when it is made. This is the companion to the head-and-shoulder move. The count for a right-handed person is (1) foot, head, and shoulders left, (2) come back right (short step), (3) short step with the left foot as the ball is crossed over in front of the body from right to left, and (4) bring the right foot across and go to the basket.

Crossover Dribble

A crossover or switch dribble is a basic move used in the open court when there is sufficient room between the dribbler and defender and the dribbler has momentum (Figure 3.15). In this dribble, the ball is pushed low and quickly across the body. The proper technique is to push the ball from right to left (or vice versa) as a zigzag move from right to left (or vice versa) is made. This move is used when the defender overplays the path of the dribbler on the ball side. Teach players to make the move before a defender gets too close.

Spin Dribble

A spin or whirl dribble is used for maximum ball protection when the ballhandler is closely guarded. During this move the body is kept between ball and defender as shown in Figure 3.16. The disadvantage of this move is that the ballhandler loses sight of defenders and teammates briefly and may be susceptible to blind side traps or double teams. Spin-dribble footwork uses quick stop, rear-turn pivot, and zigzag moves from right to left (or vice versa). As the 270 degree rear turn is made on the left (or right) foot the right (left) hand pulls the ball with the pivot

Figure 3.14 Head-and-shoulders crossover: weight on right foot, dribble ball on right side (a); zigzag on left foot (b); weight back to right foot (c); cross ball over in front of body from right to left (d); and head to basket (e).

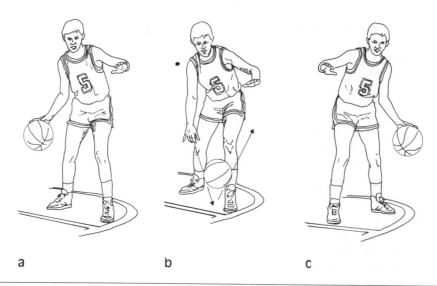

a   b   c

Figure 3.15 Crossover dribble: low dribble (one hand; a); crossover low and in front of body (b); and low dribble (opposite hand; c).

a   b

c   d

Figure 3.16 Spin or whirl dribble: low dribble, quick stop (a); rear turn (b); pull ball (keep it in the holster and on the hip; c); and change hands and move past defender (d).

until the turn is completed and the first step is made with the right (or left) foot. The ball is kept close to the body—the pull is similar to pulling a pistol from a holster. Have players pull the ball and keep it tight to avoid defenders' reach- or slap-around moves. After the rear turn is completed the ball is switched to the opposite hand and full-court vision is regained. This move changes direction from an angle that is forward right to forward left (or vice versa) as the ball is changed from the right hand to the left hand (or vice versa).

Rocker Dribble

The rocker dribble or backup dribble move is used to back away from trouble, defensive traffic, or a trap (Figure 3.17). When dribbling with the right (left) hand, players should break down into a control-dribble position with the left (right) foot forward, then explode back in a sliding movement to get away from the defense. After reestablishing a gap on the defense any dribble move may be used to penetrate or go by the defender. The crossover dribble is especially effective following the dribble rocker.

Behind-the-Back Dribble

One of the most popular dribble moves is the behind-the-back dribble. It is used to change hands (usually from the preferred hand to the nonpreferred hand) and go past a defender who is overplaying on the right (left). This is done by changing direction slightly to the left (right) and going by on the dribbler's left (right). As the left (right) foot moved forward, the ball is moved from right to left (or vice versa) behind the back, coming up under the left (right) hand for a continuation of the dribble. The coordination of the dribble and footwork can be carried out by a stationary yo-yo V; players dribble with one hand back and forth with the opposite foot forward. When the ball is controlled from front to back it can be moved behind the back as a step is taken with the left foot (Figure 3.18).

Between-the-Legs Dribble

The between-the-legs dribble is used to avoid overplay and to change the ball from one hand to the other. When the ball is being dribbled with the right hand, it can be changed to the left hand and between the legs when the left or right foot is forward (best with the right foot forward). This move is reversed for a left-hand dribble. The ball is kept low and crossed over between the legs with a quick, hard push across (Figure 3.19). The coordination of the dribble and the footwork can be learned by walking forward

a   b

Figure 3.17 Rocker dribble: when in the trap use low dribble (a) and sliding steps backward (b) to get out.

Figure 3.18 Behind-the-back dribble—right-to-left-hand move: dribble with right hand (a), move left foot forward (b), move ball from right to left behind back (c and d), and continue dribble with left hand, moving past defender (e).

Figure 3.19 Between-the-legs dribble: dribble with right hand (a), push between the legs when one foot is forward (b), and change to left hand (c).

slowly as the ball is crossed over between the legs during each step.

```
╔════════════════════════════════════╗
║        COACHING POINTS             ║
║         FOR DRIBBLING              ║
╠════════════════════════════════════╣
║                                    ║
║  • Keep your head up. See the whole floor. ║
║  • Control the ball with the fingers and the ║
║    pads of the hands.             ║
║  • Use a quick stop when ending the ║
║    dribble.                        ║
║                                    ║
╚════════════════════════════════════╝
```

BALLHANDLING DRILLS

MOVING PAIRS PASSING

Purpose: To teach partner passing and catching skills while moving and when playing against a defender.

Equipment: One ball and floor space of 15 to 20 feet in diameter per pair of players.

Procedure: Organize pairs of players with a ball and a court area—one passer and one receiver. The receiver gets open, receives the pass with feet in the air, quick-stops, catches the ball and faces the passer in a triple-threat position. The passer then becomes the next receiver. The drill involves continuous passing and catching (Figure 3.20). All passing and catching rules are practiced.

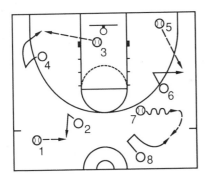

Figure 3.20 Line drill: passing/catching.

WALL PASSING

Purpose: To teach players the individual ballhandling skills of passing and catching without a teammate.

Equipment: One ball per player and a wall space or tossback rebounding device.

Procedure: All basic passes can be practiced against a wall. A target may also be added. The tossback, a commercial rebound device, has been found to be especially helpful for practicing this skill. It rewards a good pass by returning the ball on target and informs the athlete when an inaccurate pass is made. The following passes should be practiced: chest, bounce, overhead, baseball, and push. Remember to have players pass the ball with feet on the floor and catch the ball with feet in the air.

DRIBBLING

Purpose: To teach ballhandling skills of dribbling.

Equipment: One ball per line (minimum) on a half court (minimum).

Procedure: Using the line drill formation, four lines of players are formed on the baseline. The dribble moves of the drill are then practiced for one circuit. Players concentrate on maintaining eye contact with the basket at the opposite end of the court.

Options:
- Speed dribble—Players dribble down the court with one hand, then return the ball with the other hand.
- Change-of-pace dribble—Players alternate speed and control dribbles down the court, using the opposite hand on return.

Chapter 4

Shooting

Shooting is probably the best known fundamental skill—every player you coach is interested in scoring. If simply given a basket and a ball, even a novice will invariably dribble and shoot.

Shooting is a skill that can be practiced alone and one that produces immediate feedback. It is the fundamental skill that players enjoy and practice most. Most coaches contend that all players can become good shooters because good shooters are only made through long hours, days, and eventually years of practice. It should also be recognized that great shooters must also possess some very special physical talents. Any player, however, can become a good shooter and an excellent free throw shooter.

One of the two basic objectives of basketball is getting a good shot in order to score a basket. The other objective is preventing an opponent from doing the same. This chapter contains guidelines for teaching players how to get a good shot on every attempt.

FIELD GOAL SHOOTING

It is important to teach each player to become a scorer, not just a shooter. Anyone can shoot but considerable skill is required to score consistently in game situations. In order to maximize their shooting-to-scoring ratio, players

---

> **COACHING POINTS**
> **FOR GENERAL SHOOTING**
>
> - Balance and quickness
> - Rhythm
> - Follow-through
> - Quickness without hurrying
> - Vertical alignment
> - Physical and mental practice

must learn when to shoot and when to pass, what their range is, and from what spots on the court they can consistently make field goals. The recommended minimal percentage guidelines are shown in Table 4.1.

It is important for players to develop a proper shooting attitude. This consists of concentrating on each shot attempt by focusing on

Table 4.1 Desired Field Goal Percentages

Grade level	Practice %	Game %
Elementary	35	30
Junior high school	40	35
Senior high school	45	40
College	50	45
Professional	55	50

the target and visualizing the perfect shot every time. They must learn to ignore distractions and see only the ball and net in their minds. It is also necessary to build confidence over a period of time—this can be aided by players' developing self-talk. Self-feedback is provided on each shot—successful shots are remembered and reinforced while missed shots are analyzed and forgotten. For example, comments such as "great shot" on a make or "off balance to the left" on a miss might be appropriate self-talk on shot attempts. Players should never be too hard on themselves for a missed shot—it is more productive to evaluate the error and then forget it.

Practice can make a shooter into a scorer—this is the secret of good shooting. Have players spend ample time shooting with proper form. Practice makes permanent (not perfect); therefore players must learn to practice game shots at game spots at game speed. It is also helpful to use mental practice—have them regularly spend 3 to 5 minutes visualizing successful shooting situations and specific shots.

Proper shooting technique can only be developed if basic skills and strength are sufficient. Use a smaller ball and lower basket for teaching shooting skills before grade 7 (ages 11-12). Proper mechanics can be learned early, in grades 4 through 6 (ages 9-11), and readily transferred to a regulation ball and basket.

Passing and quick stops are the most important shooting fundamentals. Players should learn to get the shot by first moving to get open. Then they must catch and face in triple-threat position and be prepared to shoot.

Teach players to attack and get shots as close to the basket as possible on a dribble drive. They should challenge the defense by probing for the basket—the ultimate shot is the lay-up.

Players should strive to become shooting ROBOTs—scoring machines. A good shot means these things:

- **R**—A player is in effective scoring range.
- **O**—A good shot requires that the shooter be open.

- **B**—A good shot is always taken on balance.
- **O**—Good shots are one-count shots where a player's feet are ready and the ball is shot in a single positive motion to the basket from the shooting pocket.
- **T**—No teammate has a better shot.

Shooting Lay-Ups

All players should learn to shoot both left- and right-handed lay-ups. The technique is to jump from the left leg when shooting right-handed and vice versa when shooting left-handed. A high jump is made by "stamping" on the last step to minimize the forward long jump. Have players use the backboard whenever possible; exceptions may be the baseline dribble drive and the dunk shot. The dunk shot should be used only when a player can dunk the ball without strain and there is minimal defensive traffic.

The Approach

Attacking or accelerating to the basket is a positive approach that your players can readily use. When shooting a lay-up, the attack move is made by taking the ball up with two hands (bring the free hand to the ball when dribbling, chin, and keep the ball chest high on the side away from the defender). Players should keep the ball away from the hip. The last dribble is timed with the step on the inside foot when using a dribble-drive move. Teach beginners to use a "gallop" move with a lay-up. For a right-handed dribbler and shooter the last one-two gallop move will be with the right foot and left foot, in that order.

The Jump

The knee is then raised high when jumping and straightened just before the peak of the jump (Figure 4.1). Other tips for players include using the backboard to their advantage, shooting softly with a feather touch, and focusing on the ball and the target.

The types of lay-ups to teach are the overhand or push (palm facing target—Figure 4.2) and the underhand or scoop lay-up which

Figure 4.1 The peak of the jump.

produces a softer shot and is shot with palm up (Figure 4.3).

Set and Jump Shot Techniques

The movements for shooting the one-hand set shot and jump shot are the same. The essential difference between the two shots is that the jump shot is executed by shooting the set shot just before the peak of a jump.

Proper shooting mechanics should be taught and practiced. The medium arc shot (about 60 degrees at the angle of release) is the best compromise between the best arc for shooting (a trajectory that is almost vertical) and the available strength for accurate shooting. The shooting foot, elbow, wrist, and hand are all in the same vertical plane with the basket as the ball is brought up past the face. As was stated before, the hand and arm motions are the same on all set or jump shots—the power comes from the legs. Backspin on the ball produced by finger thrust increases the angle of rebound off the rim (i.e., it produces a more vertical bounce) and gives the shot a greater chance of going in.

Figure 4.2 Lay-up—overhand or push.

In addition to these general points of shooting mechanics, players should be taught specific fundamentals such as proper body position, holding the ball, and the different steps of executing the shot.

Figure 4.3 Lay-up—underhand or scoop.

Balance

A shooter needs to be on balance because a good shot starts from the floor up. The feet should be ready, and the player should get into basic position and face the basket.

Grip

The next step is for the shooter to grip the ball properly. The fingers of the shooting hand should be spread comfortably with the ball touching the whole hand except the heel (Figure 4.4). This is done by placing the ball in the shooting hand while holding the palm up in front of the body (Figure 4.5). The balance hand should be kept on the side or under the ball to avoid thumb drag. When handling the ball, players can move it to shooting position by grasping the ball with both hands on the side and then rotating the ball.

Figure 4.4 Shooting hand grip: use the whole hand (except for the heel).

Figure 4.5 Grip of shooting hand (use whole hand).

Wrist

After moving the ball into shooting position the shooter should cock the wrist back and lock it. This position is illustrated in Figure 4.6.

Figure 4.6 Lock and cock wrist.

Elbow

The elbow is kept up, in, and in front of the wrist (Figure 4.7). Beginners may have a lower starting elbow position, but the elbow should still be in front of the wrist. The ball is kept close and steadied by the balance hand. Figure 4.8 shows correct shooting position.

Target

Focusing on a specific target on the rim or backboard is essential to shooting. For angled shots, the target on the backboard is the upper corner of the rectangle on the same side the shot is taken. The target should be hit on the way down. For straighter shots, the target is the rim or ring. When the basket ring is the target, the shooter should focus on the middle eyelet on the back of the rim. A shot aimed in this manner may still be successful even if it is short or otherwise not completely accurate.

Release

Shooting up and over requires thrusting the fingers up and forward through the ball. Have players visualize shooting out of the

Figure 4.7 Elbow up, in, and in front of wrist.

Figure 4.8 Triple-threat ball position—correct for shooting.

Figure 4.9 Thrust up and over (check backspin by shooting a vertical shot).

velop their sense of where the line is without looking down. Long shots will produce long rebounds and rebounding teammates must adjust accordingly. Knowing the time and score is important for all shots but especially the three-point shot. This shot should only be attempted as the player is moving toward the line with a quick stop or after a plant and pivot. These movements will provide the greater force needed for this shot and allow

top of a glass telephone booth or over a seven-foot defender. Backspin will be produced on the ball if the fingers thrust the ball up and over (Figure 4.9).

Follow-Through

The final step in shooting is to follow through with complete elbow extension, arm pronation or turnout and wrist flexion (controlled relaxation). Players should visualize putting the fingers in a cookie jar, putting a hand in the basket, or making a parachute with the floating hand and holding it (Figure 4.10).

The Three-Point Shot

Shooting the three-point shot requires some adjustment. Three-point shooters must de-

Figure 4.10 Follow through (complete extension and pronation of arm).

beginning players to take it without straining. Emphasis should be placed on bending the knees more for extra power from the legs and on releasing the shot on the way up. It is more of a set shot.

Post Hook-Shot Principles

This shot is used by players who receive the ball in a low post position with their backs to the basket. The best location for a post shot is just outside the free throw lane near the block (Figure 4.11). This low-medium post position is taken just outside the lane near the first or second free throw lane spaces.

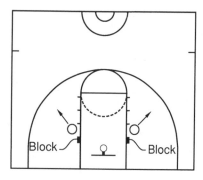

Figure 4.11 Posting up on the blocks.

The offensive player has the ball in the low post area with the ball under the chin. Any player receiving a pass should be in basic position. The footwork for the post shot involves making a rear-turn pivot into the lane using the baseline foot as the pivot foot. The other foot is used to step into the lane as far as possible in the balanced position. Ideally, this foot is parallel to the baseline (left foot in Figure 4.12). When the nonpivot foot hits the floor, the pivot foot is raised as the opposite knee is lifted high and rotated as in a normal lay-up. The ball is then moved from the chinning position past the side of the head, pushed overhead, and released with full arm extension and pronation. The move is led by the inside elbow.

The complete post shot sequence is illustrated in the figure and includes these essential steps:

- Chin the ball.
- Make a rear turn and step across.

COACHING POINTS FOR FIELD GOAL SHOOTING

- Have feet and hands ready
- Start shots on the floor; emphasize footwork
- Practice rim and board shots
- Practice game shots at game spots at game speed
- Practice shooting from spots, the pass, and the dribble

- Move the ball up and over with full extension and pronation and keep the ball close to the body.
- Rotate and shoot the post shot.
- Land in basic position and assume the shot will be missed.

FREE THROW SHOOTING

Free throw shooting can be improved by acting on the following suggestions. Your team must practice free throws in proportion to their scoring importance in a game (approximately 20%). For practices evenly divided between defense and offense, this means that 10% of total practice time should be spent on free throws. In a 2-hour practice session this would mean at least 10 minutes spent solely on free throw practice. Because free throw shooting is a skill that must be practiced constantly if it is to be maintained, set up a plan for players to practice free throw shooting in the off-season.

Game percentage goals as shown in Table 4.2 should be set relative to age level.

Table 4.2 Desired Free Throw Percentage

Grade level	Practice %	Game %
Elementary	55	50
Junior high school	65	60
Senior high school	75	70
College	80	75
Professional	85	80

Figure 4.12 The post shot: meet and chin the ball—use the quick stop (a). Step into lane, parallel to baseline (b). Protect the ball (c). Take the ball up and over (d). Follow through, face the basket, and assume the shot will be missed (e).

Practice standards should be 5% higher than game goals because of normal game performance slippage.

Confidence

Develop confidence in free throw shooting with a gradual, long-term approach. Players need to groove the shot early in practice and during the season. This is done by having them shoot consecutive free throws. Teach them to concentrate on every shot using positive thoughts, such as making the opponents pay for every foul, thinking net (shots that hit only net), and seeing the net ripple as the ball goes through. A positive shooting attitude is also developed by praising successful shots and evaluating missed shots. The shooter blocks out all negative thoughts and uses only the positive ones.

Elementary age players should use a smaller ball, lower baskets (9 feet), and a shorter free throw line (9 feet).

Free Throw Techniques

The key differences with regard to field goal shooting are alignment (foot position), keeping the weight forward, focusing on the same specific target each shot, pausing at the bottom of the shot, and establishing a ritual.

The complete free throw technique is shown in Figure 4.13.

Players should know how a good shot looks and feels and be able to shoot free throws with eyes closed. A shot should be executed with controlled tension—not too relaxed or too tight.

Align

The shooting foot, elbow, hand, and ball are aligned in a vertical plane with the basket. The alignment of the shooting foot should be in the same spot every time and pointed toward the basket or slightly to the left of a line perpendicular to the free throw line. The balance foot is about 15 to 18 degrees to the left.

Grip

The ball is on the whole shooting hand, with the balance hand on the side or under ball.

Wrist

Free throw shooters should cock the wrist back and lock it in place, much as they would for a set shot.

Elbow

Keep the elbow in close to the body, up, and in front of the wrist.

Weight Forward

Shooters should assume a modified basic position with weight over the front foot, hold the head steady, and keep the back straight.

Aim

The focus should be on the center eyelet in the back of the rim. A player should fix on

a   b   c

Figure 4.13 The free throw: get down with weight forward (a). Pause at the bottom of the shot (b). Follow through (c).

the net and think "make them pay." The focus on the target should continue until the ball goes through the net.

Pause

At the bottom of the shot the player should pause until physically and mentally calm and focused, but no longer. After the pause, all motion should be up and over toward the basket.

Follow-Through

Full extension and pronation are keys to the follow-through. The shooter should come up off the floor—get power from the legs. The upper arm should be at 30-35 degrees from the vertical on the follow-through.

Ritual

A ritual should be developed for the complete shot. Help each player do the same thing the same way, every time. It is much easier to groove a pattern that is always the same. A deep breath just before the shot should always be part of the ritual.

**COACHING POINTS
FOR FREE THROW SHOOTING**

- Begin in a low position on every shot (align)
- Move weight forward, follow through
- Pause at the bottom of each shot
- Develop and follow a ritual
- Keep it simple and do it the same each time

SHOOTING DRILLS

LINE SHOOTING ADDITION

Purpose: To teach shooting in a simulated game situation.

Equipment: Half court (minimum), four balls (minimum).

Procedure: Form groups of players in the four lines on the baseline formation. This is a form shooting exercise without the ball or a defender (the ball is added later). Players should execute a quick stop in shooting position after jumping from the foot closest to the basket. Later, the drill may be done using a ball and an underhand spin pass or a dribble.

Options:

- Straight line—Shots are taken without a target at the free throw lines and half-court line with players focusing on the basket at the opposite end of the floor.
- Offensive zigzag—A shot is taken at the location of each change of direction spot. Most movement should be lateral to make it easier for players to select the foot closest to the basket.
- Straight line with shots called by the coach—Players in groups of four begin on the command "go," next four players begin when there is 15 to 18 feet of space between them and the preceding group, coach designates basket to side of court (intersection of sideline and half-court line may be used), players move forward under control in basic position until coach gives the command "pass"; at that time each player on the court simulates catching a pass with a quick stop and a shot to imaginary basket. On the command "go" all players continue up the court until the coach throws another imaginary pass; players must be ready to shoot with balance and control at any time, going down shooting to the right, coming back shooting to the left.

FIELD GOAL PROGRESSION

Purpose: To progressively self-teach the skill of shooting with a drill that provides a player with feedback needed for improving shooting in all basketball situations.

Equipment: One ball per player (when possible), basket.

Procedure: Each player will take a basketball and review shooting by following this shooting progression. Ten repetitions of each of the options are carried out each time.

Options:

- Two-hand ball slaps develop the feel of having the ball in the whole hand.
- Form shots are one-handed vertical shots without a target starting with ball in the hand in palm-up position, and rotating it into the shooting pocket with the other hand behind the back.
- Close shots taken with a target (rim and backboard) remind players to practice from the inside out, starting close to the basket and gradually moving out.
- Circle shots is a drill in which each player will move in a circle, holding the ball with two hands chest high, using proper quick stop footwork while shooting at five spots inside the free throw lane as shown in Figure 4.14. After five shots are taken moving clockwise, have each player shoot five shots moving counterclockwise. Shots taken at 45 degrees are board shots (#2, #4). No dribbling is allowed—Circle shots focus on having the feet in position and hands ready to handle the ball.

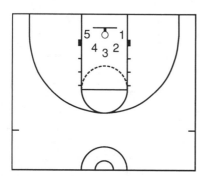

Figure 4.14 Circle shots: targets at five locations inside the lane.

- Shooting from a pass involves players tossing a two-hand underhand pass to themselves in a desired spot and using proper footwork to get to that spot and take a spot shot.
- From a triple-threat position 15 to 20 feet from the basket, a player makes a dribble-drive move to the left or right, makes a quick stop, and shoots from a desired spot.

Preliminary work should be done on pickup ''technique.'' This can be done by having players throw the spin pass to themselves or having them take the last dribble with either hand, jumping from the opposite foot with a quick stop at the same time and landing in triple-threat position.

PAIRS OR IN-AND-OUT SHOOTING

Purpose: To teach shooting in a two-on-zero game simulation drill that covers all shooting situations.

Equipment: Basket and one ball per pair of players (players can also work in groups of 3 or 4).

Procedure: This continuous competitive-shooting drill, shown in Figure 4.15, incorporates all principles of movement: passing and catching, shooting, and offensive rebounding. Players are grouped in pairs (there may be one or two pairs per basket). The basic rules are:

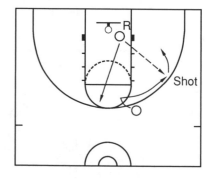

Figure 4.15 Pairs shooting: one pass.

- All pairs begin on coach's command, starting with rebounder under the basket with a ball; teammate gets open for shot, calls rebounder's name, and receives a pass for the shot.
- Shooters rebound their own shots until a basket is made (always assuming the shot will be missed), then gain possession for pass to teammate for a shot.
- Receiver must always get open and call passer's name.
- Passers make a quick, on target pass at the right time and with trickery to teammate for a good shot and go quickly

to another location near the edge of the power zone, ready to move only when teammate has scored and has possession of the ball.

Options:

- Groove: Each player gets open and shoots for 30 seconds while teammate rebounds; players take turns shooting and rebounding, changing every 30 seconds.
- Shooter makes five baskets and switches positions with teammate.
- The 10-shot game to 10 made baskets involves players moving with shots from pass and from a dribble.
- The coach designates the type of pass and type of shot (regular, jab fake, and shot).
- Pressuring the shooter involves making a poor defensive closeout and applying some type of false pressure (go by, shout, hand in face, contact) after the pass to the shooter. Defender cannot block or alter the shot or foul the shooter. At least once a week use the variation of having defenders pressure shooters with hands up to help shooters develop the greater arch needed for shooting over defenders.
- Three-pass shooting involves shooting from an outlet pass (passer posts up), a pass to post (passer cuts), and a return pass for shot (Figure 4.16).

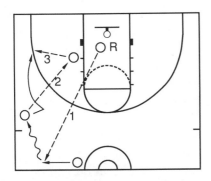

Figure 4.16 Pairs shooting: three passes.

- The *beat-the-star* variation places shooters in competition with a designated star shooter with a rebounder partner. Game begins with one free throw and con-

tinues with players shooting set or jump shots. Scoring rules for free throws give challengers 1 point for successful shots and 3 points for star on misses; challengers score 1 point for successful field goals and star gets 2 points for misses. The game can be played to 11 or 21 points.

"MAKE IT–TAKE IT" ROW-SHOOTING DRILL

Purpose: To teach the skill of shooting in a self-testing format adjusted to standards set by the coach.

Equipment: Basket and one ball per player.

Procedure: All tasks in this drill are self-testing. They require the player to meet effective scoring standards. All moves are to be carried out consecutively without rest to practice shooting in game situations.

Players make dribble-drive lay-up moves (Figure 4.17) from left and right corners (with foot on sideline), each hash mark, and the top of the key. They are allowed only one dribble and must make three baskets in a row from each spot. Frontcourt players with the ability to dunk the ball must do so by dribbling only once. The objective is to cover the greatest distance possible with a lay-up scoring move. After each row of three shots is made, the player earns the right to shoot free throws. The percentage goal must be met on free throws (4 of 5 for college players; 3 of 4 for high school; 2 of 3 for junior high) or the player repeats the move and free throw group.

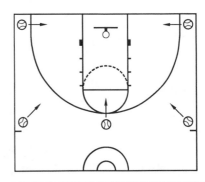

Figure 4.17 Dribble-drive starting spots.

Shooters take jump and set shots from five selected spots with spin pass moves and dribble moves to the left and the right. The same field goal shooting objectives must be met—3 in a row (abbreviated *row 3*) at each spot. This is immediately followed by five, four, or three free throws (depending on the age level). If the free throw objective is not met, the move and free throw group must be repeated. Be sure to include backboard shots.

Options:

- Dribble Drive—row 3:
  Left corner/free throws.
  Left hash mark/free throws.
  Top of the key/free throws.
  Right hash mark/free throws.
  Right corner/free throws.
  —15 field goals/25 free throws
- Spin-pass field goals—row 3:
  Game shots/game spots/game speed.
  —15 field goals/25 free throws.
- Field goals from the dribble—row 3:
  Game shots/game spots/game speed.
  —15 field goals/25 free throws.

Note: Inside players should substitute inside moves for shots from the dribble. A variation of the free throw requirement can be substituted where row free throws are used (college—4 in a row, high school—3, junior high school—2, elementary school—make 1). An adjustment in shooting distance should also be made for younger players.

FREE THROW SHOOTING DRILLS

Purpose: To develop free throw scoring skill to meet age-group standards.

Equipment: Ball and basket.

Procedure: Free throw practice should include physical and mental practice. It should be done in the following sequence:

First, players should groove the free throw by shooting consecutive shots. It is recommended that each player make 20 free throws before each practice session and keep records of the number of attempts. It is also helpful to keep records of the maximum number of consecutive free throws made in a practice situation and place players in the "10" club, the "25" club, the "50" club, and the "Century" club (100 free throws in a row).

Mental practice is used any time a player is waiting to shoot free throws on the court and for any 5-minute period off the court. Have players focus mentally on required steps and visualize perfect performance.

Set up a system of scrimmage shots requiring players not actively playing to make 5 to 10 free throws before they are allowed to substitute.

Competition shooting places groups of players in various competitive situations.

Feeling the shot involves shooting free throws with eyes closed. Players work in pairs and partner provides exact information on shot location. This is done once a week for a 5-minute period. Shots are usually taken in sets of three. Goals might be 1 of 2, 2 of 3, or row 2, 3, 4.

Options:

- Row free throws involve making a given number of consecutive free throws. For example, coaches might require from 3 to 8 in a row. A variation of this game is called team free throws. The group of 12 to 16 players is divided into a team of 6 to 8 at the two main baskets on a court. They remain at that basket and shoot free throws one at a time until each player, in order, makes a successful shot. At that time the teams switch baskets and repeat the process.
- Set up competition for the number of row free throws a group of 2, 3, or 4 players can make in a designated period of time. Players shoot one-shot, one-and-one–shot (they must make the first to shoot the second), or two-shot situations. A 5-minute period is ideal for this variation.

- Net shots is a shooting game to a designated number of points in a designated time. Count 2 points for a net shot, 1 point for a rim hit that is made and take away 2 points for a miss.

FOUNDATION 500

Purpose: To develop shooting skill in the off-season or outside of team practice situation.

Equipment: Ball and basket.

Procedure: Each player shoots the following:

1. One hundred free throws (10 with eyes closed until ball is released).
2. One hundred foundation shots, broken down as follows:

   - Ten form shots consisting of perfect shots taken overhead, against a wall, or against the backboard without shooting at a target.
   - Fifty close shots taken in the free throw lane 6 feet from the basket in all possible locations, including the 45-degree angle backboard shot.
   - Ten mental shots where players visualize 10 specific game shots (free throw and field goals) in key situations. Have players practice making perfect shots and shutting out all errors from the mind.
   - Thirty choice shots to help players groove a favorite shot.
3. One hundred shots by players from a spin pass to themselves, including stationary spot shots in the locations, positions, and range that each player will use against all types of defenses.
4. One hundred shots from a spin pass moving left (50) and moving right (50).
5. One hundred shots taken off the dribble (50 to the right and 50 to the left).

Note: The tossback rebound device may be used instead of the spin-pass technique—it is an excellent self-teaching device for learning to shoot from a pass. This is an often neglected skill or weakness with individual players.

Chapter 5

Outside Moves:
Playing the Perimeter

Any discussion of individual offensive moves should begin with the reminder that basketball is first and foremost a team sport. So while every game situation will provide opportunities for individuals to use offensive moves while they have the ball, the player with the ball must closely coordinate offensive moves with four other players. As coach you will need to place certain limitations on individual offensive moves.

Outside moves are, of course, offensive moves around the periphery of the court. There are four types of individual outside moves:

- Live ball moves (when the offensive player with the ball still has a dribble available)
- Dribbling moves (when the offensive player is in the process of dribbling)
- Dead ball moves (made at the completion of the dribble when a player has used the dribble and stopped in possession of the ball)
- Completion shots (shots taken after a dribble)

FUNDAMENTALS OF LIVE BALL MOVES

All live ball moves begin from a basic position with the player in triple-threat position facing the basket. The preferred way to get into position is to catch the ball with the feet in the air and to land using a quick stop facing the basket. The alternative is to catch and face, that is, to catch the ball with both hands, quick-stop, and pivot in triple-threat position to face the basket.

The player should protect the ball and keep it close to the body, using the body as a shield. The player provides this protection in triple-threat position by keeping the ball near and under the shoulder during a live ball move (Figure 5.1), by dribbling the ball on the side opposite the defender, by using a chinit and pivot technique in defensive traffic (Figure 5.2), and by avoiding dangling the ball with elbows extended.

Conserving time and space is a basic guideline for outside moves with the ball. All moves should be quick, and made in a straight line toward the basket whenever

Figure 5.1 Triple-threat position.

Figure 5.2 Chinit and pivot.

possible. The offensive player should make slight contact with the defender while moving past on the dribble drive and use quick pass and shot fakes while maintaining basic position. The live ball move (using the dribble drive past a defender) should be made with a quick first step past the defender toward the basket.

The attack-the-front-foot rule is applied when the defender is in a staggered stance (see Figure 5.3). The most vulnerable side of the defender is the front-foot side, because the defender must pivot before angling back to cut off penetration by the offensive player. So the offensive player should be aware of the defender's front foot and use a live ball move to

that side of the body whenever possible.

The player should attack the basket on the dribble drive by accelerating to the basket under control. "Now or never" means that the live ball move is best made immediately after the player receives a pass, before the defense can adjust and while the defense is moving. If in doubt, the player should pass the ball.

The objective of any live ball move in the power zone is to score a lay-up with one dribble (seldom are more than two dribbles needed). But players should read the defense to anticipate chances to use a controlled dribble drive as a reaction to a defensive adjustment. Learning to control the dribble drive well enough to permit a last-second pass to an open teammate will help players challenge the defense even more.

Permanent Pivot Foot Moves

These moves should be used when a primary pivot foot is used for all live ball moves. The left foot should be used for right-handed players and vice versa. The moves that should be taught are the direct drive, the hesitation move, the rocker step, and the crossover step. NO·DIDDLEY-DUO-

Direct Drive

This is a drive past the defender with the dominant foot. The right-handed player should drive past the defender's left side taking the first step with the right foot (and vice versa) by establishing triple-threat position in a staggered stance, and pushing off the pivot (LEFT) foot. The quick move is taken with the free foot straight to the basket, as the ball is pushed to the floor and in front before the pivot foot is lifted. Finally, a step is taken past the defender with the permanent pivot foot to attack the basket. The breakdown count consists of (a) the explosion step with the dominant foot, and (b) pushing the ball ahead to the floor on the dribble drive (Figure 5.4).

Hesitation or Step-Step Move

This is a dominant-side move, made after a jab step to test the defender's reaction. It is

a   b

Figure 5.3 Defender in staggered stance (a). Drive past defender on the front foot side (defender must pivot to cut off move; b).

Figure 5.4 First step past the defender—brush the shoulder.

done by establishing triple-threat position and making a short "jab" step at the defender and basket with dominant foot. If the defender doesn't react to the jab step, a second "explosion" step can be made past the defender. The breakdown count consists of (a) a jab step with a short pause, (b) a long explosion step, and (c) a dribble drive initiated by pushing the ball ahead to the floor (Figure 5.5).

Rocker Step

Another dominant-side move is the rocker step, a direct-drive fake and return to triple-threat position, followed by a direct-drive move. The sequence is to establish triple-

threat position, make a short jab step direct drive, then return to triple-threat position. When the defender moves toward the offensive player in reaction to the return to triple-threat position, the offensive player should then make a direct-drive move. The breakdown count consists of (a) jab step (down), (b) rock back to triple threat (up), (c) explosion step (down), and (d) dribble drive (go) started by pushing the ball ahead to the floor (Figure 5.6).

Crossover Step

This is the basic countermove to the opposite side when the defender overplays the dominant side. It consists of establishing triple-threat position, making a short jab step toward the defender, crossing the dominant foot over to the other side of and past the defender while keeping the ball close to the body and swinging it across at the same time. The ball then is pushed ahead to the floor to begin the dribble drive. The dominant foot is pointed toward the basket. Players should keep the pivot foot stationary while both the jab step and crossover step are made with the same foot. The breakdown count consists of (a) making a jab step, (b) swinging the dominant foot and the ball over to the other side, and (c) pushing the ball ahead to the floor on the dribble drive (Figure 5.7). The ball should be moved across high or low, in the chest or knee area.

Figure 5.5 Hesitation or step-step move: short first step (a), and long second step past defender (b).

Figure 5.6 Rocker step: jab fake (down; a); return to triple-threat position with shot fake (up; b); and take long first step past defender reacting to shot fake (down; c).

The direct-drive, hesitation, rocker-step, and crossover moves are the basic four live ball moves needed to combat most defenders. These moves are sufficient for most beginning players.

Either Pivot Foot Moves

These moves are taught when either foot is used as the pivot foot for live ball moves.

Both right- and left-handed players should be able to establish a pivot foot with either foot when this method is chosen.

Direct Drive Direction Foot

This move used to dribble drive past a defender consists of making the explosion step with the foot on the side the player is driving. The sequence is to make a quick stop facing the basket, and, when driving right, use the

Figure 5.7 Crossover step: short first step (jab; a), and crossover ball and free foot (move past defender; b).

left foot for a pivot foot, and take an explosion step past the defender with the right foot. Also, when driving left, step with the left foot using the right foot as the pivot foot. The ball is pushed ahead on the floor on the dribble drive. The breakdown count consists of (a) an explosion step with the foot on the same side as the dribble drive (right foot to right side, left foot to left side) and (b) pushing the ball ahead to the floor to start the dribble drive.

Direct Drive Opposite Foot

This move is used to drive past a defender on either side by using the opposite foot to step across and shielding the ball as a direct drive is made. The "opposite drive" is executed by making a quick stop facing the basket, and, when driving right, stepping past the defender with a left-foot explosion step and pushing the ball ahead on the dribble drive. The breakdown count consists of (a) taking an explosion step past the defender with the foot opposite the side of the dribble drive, and (b) pushing the ball ahead on the floor for the dribble drive (Figure 5.8).

Crossover

Players should also learn a countermove using either foot as the pivot foot (fake right,

Figure 5.8 Either pivot foot live ball move—direct drive with opposite foot. To the right with left foot (a). To the left with right foot (b).

crossover left with the left pivot foot; fake left, crossover right with the right pivot foot). This is carried out by making a quick stop facing the basket, then making a jab step and crossover with the same foot to the opposite side (swinging the ball across and close to the body), and finally pushing the ball ahead on the floor and starting a dribble drive. The breakdown count consists of (a) a jab step, (b) a crossover step with the same foot while bringing the ball across the body, and (c) a dribble drive started by pushing the ball ahead to the floor (Figure 5.9).

FUNDAMENTALS OF DRIBBLE MOVES

The dribble moves used following all live ball moves are described in detail in chapter 3—Ballhandling. Proficiency in live ball moves should be coupled with the development of quick, controlled dribble moves.

FUNDAMENTALS OF DEAD BALL MOVES

These maneuvers are used at the completion of a dribble move when the quick stop is made within 10 to 12 feet of the basket. They can be used when moving to either the left

or right, but players must be within shooting range for them to be effective.

Players in possession of the ball should avoid dead ball situations whenever possible unless a pass or shot is anticipated. In other words, the live dribble should be maintained.

Either Pivot Foot Dead Ball Moves

Jump Shot
Players should execute a quick stop and take the jump shot with balance and control (see chapter 4).

Shot Fake and Jump Shot
Players should make a quick stop and follow with a believable shot fake. The ball is moved head high while maintaining basic position with legs locked for a jump shot.

Step-Through Move
The advanced move past either side of the defender to shoot a lay-up after a quick stop (with or without a shot fake) is another attacking option. Players should make a quick stop facing the basket, followed by a shot fake to get the defender out of basic position unless the defender is already overcommitted. When going to the right, they should take a step past the defender with the left foot (or with the right foot when going left) and

a　　　　　　　　　　b

Figure 5.9 Either pivot foot live ball move—crossover drive. Crossing over from right to left (jab right; a). Driving left past defender (b).

shoot a right- (or left-) handed lay-up or post shot. The breakdown count consists of (a) shot fake, (b) step past the defender, and (c) a lay-up shot.

Crossover Move

This is an advanced countermove to step past a defender by faking one way and going the opposite for a lay-up or post shot. It is done by making a quick stop facing the basket, then taking a jab step with either foot, a crossover step and a move with the opposite foot to attempt a lay-up or post shot. The breakdown count consists of (a) jab step, (b) crossover move, and (c) lay-up or post shot.

Spinner

A pivoting rear turn and lay-up or post shot is most effective from a dead ball quick stop at right angles to the baseline when stopped by a defender in the direct path. You can teach this advanced move by having a player make a quick stop facing the sideline and the free throw lane, making a rear turn on the foot closest to the baseline, and shooting a lay-up or post shot. The breakdown count

consists of (a) making a rear turn and stepping past the defender to the basket with the opposite foot, and (b) shooting the lay-up or post shot (Figure 5.10).

FUNDAMENTALS OF COMPLETION SHOTS

All live ball moves and dribble moves should result in a pass, a dead ball move, or a completion shot. The completion shots to be developed are the basic lay-ups described in chapter 4—Shooting.

PERIMETER DRILLS

LINE LIVE BALL, DEAD BALL, COMPLETION-MOVE ADDITION

Purpose: To teach players live ball and dead ball moves and review dribble moves.

Equipment: One ball per line of players, full court.

Procedure: Form four lines of players on the baseline. No defenders are placed on the

a   b   c

Figure 5.10 Either pivot foot—dead ball. Quick stop (a). Rear turn away from defender (b). Post shot (c).

COACHING POINTS FOR OUTSIDE MOVES

Train players to follow these general points:
- Visualize the defender.
- Use game moves at game speed.
- Develop quickness and balance.
- Go at top speed under control.
- Make legal moves.
- Execute correctly, then correctly and quickly.

court. Each circuit should eventually include a beginning live ball move, dribble move(s) in the middle of the court, and a dead ball or completion move at the far basket (Figure 5.11).

SPIN PASS OUTSIDE MOVES

Purpose: To develop skill in using outside moves.

Equipment: Basket and one ball per player.

Procedure: Using a half-court area, a basketball, and a basket, have players practice live ball moves and completion or dead ball moves from a simulated pass-catching situation. Players use the two-hand underhand spin pass to themselves to begin the drill in all primary offensive locations and situations. The sequence is first to spin pass in spot locations near the edge of the power zone, catch the ball on the first

bounce with feet in the air, and land facing the basket. Players should catch and face the basket every time they handle the ball by using the quick stop and the pivot, and then attack the basket. Coaches should evaluate moves—Remember that only perfect practice makes perfect. Either permanent pivot foot or either pivot foot technique may be used for developing footwork. Using this self-monitored drill, it is possible to practice appropriate live ball, dribble, and dead ball or completion moves using the basic principles. A tossback training device may be used in conjunction with the spin pass technique to simulate passing and catching situations used with the outside moves.

CLOSEOUT—ONE-ON-ONE, TWO-ON-TWO, THREE-ON-THREE, FOUR-ON-FOUR

Purpose: To practice all outside moves by perimeter players.

Equipment: One ball and one basket per group.

Procedure: Form line of players under each basket off the court. The first player steps under the basket with the ball and will be the defender. A line of offensive players is placed 15 to 18 feet away facing the basket. The defender makes a crisp air pass to the first player in the offensive line and then closes out to defend that player. The drill begins as soon as the

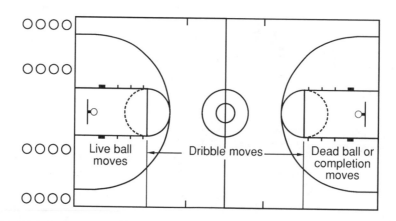

Figure 5.11 Line drill: individual outside moves.

pass is made for both offense and defense. The perimeter offensive player should read and react to the defender's actions and apply fundamentals to shoot or make an outside move.

Players may rotate to the back of the opposite line each time, play make it-take it or any arrangement of their choice. The drill may be run as a two-on-two option that then becomes a teamwork competition with on-the-ball and off-the-ball play.

Chapter 6

Inside Moves: Playing the Post

Most coaches and players recognize the importance of establishing an inside game with a post player receiving a pass near or inside the free throw lane area. This inside game can serve several useful purposes. It can produce the high percentage shot—the scoring opportunity close to the basket. The inside game can also increase opportunities for the three-point play—post players in a congested inside area are difficult to defend, and are often fouled when attempting a shot. When the ball is passed to inside post players the defense is forced to collapse in order to contain them. Passing the ball back outside to teammates can then open power zone and three-point shot opportunities.

The underlying concept in this chapter is an emphasis on another key element of the scoring objective—getting the ball inside for a higher percentage shot and forcing the defensive team to respect the inside game in order to open up outside shooting opportunities, especially the three-point field goal.

POST PLAY FUNDAMENTALS

Post play is the key to building the offense from the inside out. Playing the post is a skill

that requires a minimum of ballhandling and can be learned readily by players of all sizes with sufficient practice time and patience. Good post players get open for high-percentage shots by developing a variety of inside moves, considered "back-to-the-basket" scoring moves, usually from a low or medium post position (Figure 6.1).

Penetrate

The offensive team must penetrate the perimeter of the defense on a regular basis by taking the ball inside using the dribble drive or the pass to a post player. The objective of

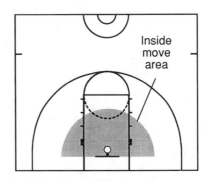

Figure 6.1 Inside move area—the low to medium post.

offensive penetration is to create the opportunity for a shot taken as close to the basket as possible, usually inside the free throw lane.

Backboard Shots

Offensive players should use the backboard when shooting after most inside moves, especially when shooting from a 45-degree angle, when using a power move, or in an offensive rebounding situation. The rule is "when going to the glass, use the glass." Chapter 4 discusses using the backboard as a target.

Assume the Miss

Since inside players are stationed close to the basket, they can be primary rebounders. Because the shooter can best gauge the exact location and timing of the shot, a post player using an inside move always assumes the shot will be missed and prepares to rebound from basic position with the elbows out and the arms and hands extended above the shoulders.

Everyone a Post

All players are post players. Though some of the best inside players have been medium- and large-sized people, technique is more important than size. A more critical factor is relative size—each player should be able to "post up" a defender of similar size or smaller.

Expect Contact

Because the inside area is frequently congested, there is often considerable physical contact. Inside players should create contact and use their bodies to control defenders. Players must learn to initiate contact while maintaining balance and basic position.

Hands Up

Passing to inside players is difficult and challenging and there is little margin for error due to congestion and time constraints. Thus, in-side players should always be prepared to receive a quick pass from a teammate by having their hands up.

Patience

Many large post players are late developers and may have a poor self-image as a result of their size and relative lack of coordination. The prescription is coaching time, patience, and regular practice.

POST SKILLS

Get your players in a post player stance. The inside or post player must develop the ability to assume an exaggerated basic position with a wider than normal base, a low center of gravity, elbows out, upper arms parallel to the floor as extensions of the shoulders, and the hands up and slightly forward with fingers spread and pointing to ceiling (Figure 6.2). Post players should provide a two-hand target for passers. The hands are kept up and ready.

Posting up takes place on the line of deployment (defined as the straight line through the ball and the basket). The inside player should attempt to get open just outside the free throw lane, near the line of deployment. Establishing position on the line of deployment shortens the distance the pass

Figure 6.2 Post player's basic stance.

from the post feeder must travel. Ideally, the post player would be posted up with shoulders square (at right angles) to the line of deployment.

Getting open at the right time is another primary task of the inside player. Because post play is a constant one-on-one battle, players must learn to create contact and stay open. Once the defender has taken a position, inside players should make contact to keep the defender in place. They should be active and use the whole body to work in a half-circle move (Figure 6.3). Hips and buttocks are used to sit on the defender's legs and maintain contact.

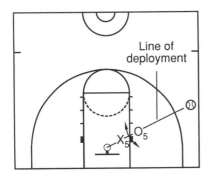

Figure 6.3 Half circle move: keep open by saddling up on defender. Feet are active.

Catching the Ball Inside

The post player should be able to locate the defender by reading the pass. The passer feeding the post player should pass to the hand target away from the closest defender. The placement of the pass will help the post player locate the defender. Keeping the passing lane open is one of the toughest tasks to teach passers. Players must keep their feet active and maintain contact until the ball is near the receiver.

Post players must step into the pass and meet the ball. They do this by catching the ball with two hands, with both feet in the air, and then executing a quick stop (except when fronted). Train players to focus on the ball until it hits their hands. When players catch a pass, they must protect the ball by using the chinit technique—elbows out, fingers up, ball under the chin. The lob or reverse can be

used when post players are fronted. When the defender establishes a ball-defender-post position, two techniques are recommended. The first is an over-the-top lob pass (Figure 6.4) where the passer shows the ball, uses a check pass to read the help-side defensive coverage, and then quickly throws a pass over the defender to the junction of the backboard and rim. The post player maintaining basic position and keeping both hands up (palms facing passer), faces the baseline and establishes contact with the defender using the hips and buttocks. The post player waits until the ball is overhead before releasing to catch the ball with two hands. The second technique is to use ball reversal to the high post or help side. If a defender is fronting on one side of the court, the ball may be reversed as the defender is sealed off and the post player steps to the ball (Figure 6.5).

Taking Out the Defender

Inside players must learn to automatically take the defender out of the play. If post players are defended on the low side, then they should take defenders lower; if fronted, they should start closer to the ball and take defenders higher. If played behind, they should step into the lane before posting up with a V-cut or rear turn. The idea is to allow the defender to take a position of choice and then take the defender further in that direction.

Reading the Defense

When the defender is fronting—playing between the passer and the post player—have your players use a lob pass over the defender or reverse the ball, pin the defender, and feed the post from the opposite side. Offensive players should use a power move or reverse lay-up on the lob play. With the defender behind a post player should catch and face using post facing moves. The post shot is also a possibility.

The defender positioned on the low side (baseline side) tells the post player to use the post or wheel move. Similarly, the power move or wheel move is indicated when the defender is positioned on the high side.

Figure 6.4 Lob pass over the defender. Both hands up—contact with rear end and hip (a). Use a check pass (pull the string) to test help-side the defender's reaction (b). Two-hand catch with power move (c).

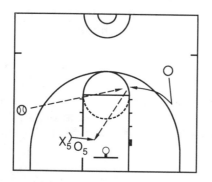

Figure 6.5 Post play: reverse the ball, pin the post defender.

Reading and reacting for the post player means learning to feel contact, reading the pass, turning to the middle, seeing the whole court, and challenging the defense.

Inside Moves

Finally, teach post players to move aggressively and be alert for open teammates. Their objective when using inside moves is to gain position for a close-in shot or to free a teammate in scoring position for a pass. This can best be achieved by mastering a variety of moves.

Post Shot

This is the move to the middle and into the free throw lane. It is the basic tool for the post player and an essential scoring weapon. The move is normally made without dribbling; the footwork and the mechanics of the post shot are explained in chapter 4—Shooting.

Power Move

The power move is usually used to the baseline side when the defender is on the high side (away from the baseline). This move may also be used toward the middle when the defender is on the baseline side. The sequence for the power move is to pivot with a rear turn on the foot closest to the defender and seal off the defensive player with the hips and buttocks. Then the post player takes one power dribble between the legs and executes a quick stop with the feet at right angles to the baseline (belly baseline). This dribble can sometimes be eliminated. Finally, the power move is used to protect the ball with the body and score with the shooting hand away from the defense; the backboard is used whenever possible (Figure 6.6).

Wheel Move

This advanced move is a power move fol-lowed by a post move. The combination is used when the defender begins by playing high-side (or low-side) defense as the power move is made but then anticipates well and cuts off the offensive player. The post player then immediately executes a post move (Fig-ure 6.7). The sequence is to initiate a power

Figure 6.6 Power move: power dribble to middle (a), quick stop (b), and power shot (c).

Figure 6.7 The wheel move can be made with the power move to the baseline (a) and post move back to the mid-dle (b) to take a shot (c).

Figure 6.8 A facing move: pivot on either foot (a), jump shot fake (b), crossover (c), and post shot (d).

move, then stop the move when the defender overreacts and then carry out a post move opposite the defender's position.

Facing Moves

These are the basic outside perimeter moves used when the defender is playing behind the post player, especially with a defensive gap. The offensive player pivots with a front turn or with a rear turn on either foot. The front-turn options are jump shot, jump shot with a shot fake, and the crossover post shot (Figure 6.8). All live ball moves may be used in this situation. Other options are the rear turn on either pivot foot followed by a jump shot, the jump shot with a shot fake, or other live ball moves. This rear turn move, first popularized by Jack Sikma, tends to clear the defender and create a gap for the quick jump shot.

COACHING POINTS FOR POST PLAY

- Teach post players inside moves they can perform with confidence and, in turn, have your team take the ball inside "in the paint" regularly so players can use these moves.
- Teach players to use the backboard on inside shots.
- Consider all players who are competitive and who like contact as potential post players.
- Have post players keep hands up inside.
- Get players in basic position with a two-hand target on the line of deployment.
- Emphasize that getting open usually requires contact and quick, strong moves.
- Train post players to read the pass, their contact with the player guarding them, and the position of other defenders.
- Teach that the post shot is the basic shot to the middle of the free throw lane and is a natural move from chinit position.
- Show post players that keeping the body between the defender and the ball during the power move is essential to its effectiveness.
- Teach players the wheel move as a power move, quick stop, and post move in sequence.
- In some situations, a post player may catch and face to use perimeter moves, especially in the free throw line/high post area.

POST DRILLS

SPIN PASS POST MOVES

Purpose: To teach players individual offensive post moves.

Equipment: Ball, basket, and optional toss-back rebound device.

Procedure: A post player uses an underhand spin pass (or pass and rebound from a tossback device) to him- or herself at a desired post location with back to the basket. Players execute three repetitions of each post move on each side of the free throw lane. The inside or low post move sequence consists of:

- Post—To the middle.
- Power—To the baseline, to the middle.
- Wheel—To the baseline, to the middle (advanced).
- Face—Jump shot, shot fake and jump shot, and crossover post move (front-turn option) or live ball move (rear-turn option).

No defender is used for this drill. The coach may also feed the post passes to check line of deployment, footwork, hand target, catching technique, and post moves.

POST PROGRESSION DRILL

Purpose: To provide players with a self-teaching progressive drill for offensive post moves.

Equipment: Ball, basket, and optional toss-back device.

Procedure: Post players begin with an underhand spin pass (or pass and rebound from a tossback) to themselves and make post moves in sequence. Five baskets are made for each move in the sequence:

- Power move—Left side, low post
- Post move—Left side, low post
- Wheel move—Left side, middle/low post
- Facing move—Left side, low post
- Facing move—High post, left elbow
- Same moves—Right side

After players make the fifth basket for each move, two consecutive successful free throws are required for them to advance to the next move (or repeat the move again).

Option:

- Require "row 3" post moves and "row 2 or 3" free throws.

TWO-ON-TWO FEED THE POST DRILL

Purpose: To teach offensive and defensive

post play skills, passing to post players, and movement after the pass for a possible return pass.

Equipment: Ball and basket, groups of four players (minimum).

Procedure: Two offensive and two defensive players work on post play from various locations around the free throw lane. All offensive and defensive post play principles are applied. When defenders obtain possession the first outlet pass or dribble for transition must be made. Have outside offensive players make a V-cut move for a possible return pass when they pass to post players.

Chapter 7

Defense

Individual defense can be a great challenge for coaches and their players. It involves developing fundamental skills that depend less on ability than determination. In addition, defense can become a consistent part of each player's game. Both mental and physical challenges await your players in developing defensive skills.

The skills that must be developed in individual defense are stance, steps, defense on and away from the ball, defensing screens, executing a defensive trap (double-team), and ''taking'' the defensive charge. These individual defensive skills are the basis for all player-to-player, zone, or combination defenses.

FUNDAMENTALS OF DEFENSE

Defense is as much a mental as a physical skill. Players should be encouraged to be proactive, rather than reactive. This can be done by emphasizing the active elements of defense represented as follows by the acronym ATTACK.

A = Attitude

The starting point of all defense is the determination to become an aggressive, intelligent defensive player. Each player must develop and maintain control of his or her playing attitude, especially on defense.

T = Teamwork

The collective effort of five defensive players is greater than five individual efforts.

T = the Tools of Defense

The three basic physical tools are the eyes, body, and feet.

A = Anticipation

Players must use basketball sense and judgment triggered by vision. They should see the ball at all times and use their eyes to anticipate.

C = Concentration

Players should be alert and ready to play defense at all times. They must assess the situation and be able to take away the opponents' strength. Players must avoid resting, physically or mentally, when playing defense.

K = Keep in Stance

Defensive players must maintain basic position at all times. They should seldom gamble by making moves that take them out of position, and all players must be constantly ready to take advantage of opponents' mistakes. Keeping in stance is the most important concept for defenders.

ESSENTIALS OF DEFENSE

In addition to being proactive defenders, players must know the nine essentials of defense: transition, purpose, pressure, position, prevention of penetration, moving, line of ball, blocking out, and communication.

Transition

The first task is to anticipate shifting from offense to defense. This requires an organized transition with communication among all five players. Players should sprint toward the defensive end of the floor but may run or slide backward once the offense is contained.

Purpose

The purpose of defense is to prevent easy scores and to gain possession of the ball through rebounds or steals. Defenders must learn to prevent situations leading to easy baskets by opponents.

Pressure

Offensive play has a basic rhythm that can be disrupted by pressure on the ball. Defensive play must maintain continuous physical and mental pressure on ballhandlers. Every shot must also be pressured physically and verbally.

Position

Train players to stay in a stance when on defense. Most fouls occur when defenders are out of position.

Prevention of Penetration

Offensive players will attempt to take the ball toward the basket by passing or dribbling.

Defenders must prevent this penetration. One defender always pressures the ball while the four other players play zone areas toward the basket to protect it and support the defender playing on the ball. Defenders should prevent middle-of-the-floor penetration toward the goal by offensive players using the dribble or direct air passes to this area when playing on-the-ball defense (especially the power zone shown in Figure 7.1). Off-the-ball defense means keeping passes out of the middle of the floor (especially the power zone) by defending zone areas toward the basket area. Defenders should play zone defense and support the defender playing on the ball.

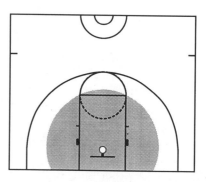

Figure 7.1 Power zone—located 15 to 18 feet from the basket.

Moving

Players must learn to move every time the ball is passed. All five players should adjust their floor position with every pass. On the ball, after the ballhandler passes the ball, the defender moves instantly toward the ball and basket. This is called jumping to the ball. When off the ball, defensive players adjust their position with every pass as well.

Line of Ball

The line of the ball principle states that players should defend their opponent only after they have taken a position ahead of the ball and toward their defensive basket. This is past the line of the ball, a side-to-side line through the ballhandler's location.

Blocking Out

Each defensive player is responsible for blocking (checking) offensive players from the basket area and gaining the defensive rebound when a shot is taken. Successful coaches recognize that defensive rebounding is an important part of team defense and devote appropriate time to teaching it.

Communication

Communication is always necessary for group success. All players must react to each other verbally and physically to produce an effective team defense. Essentially, the five players should act as one.

DEFENSE ON THE BALL

The player defending the opponent with the ball should get in and maintain a correct defensive stance. Defenders should be taught to maintain their position between the ballhandler and the basket (ball-defender-basket) as shown in Figure 7.2. The head should be kept lower than that of the offensive player with the ball, usually level with offensive player's chest.

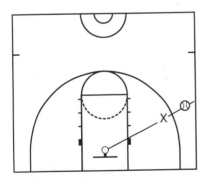

Figure 7.2 Ball-defender-basket: relative relationship of defender to basket and offensive player (with the ball) being guarded.

Guarding in a Live Ball Situation

One of the most common, important, and difficult tasks players will face on defense is defending a player who still has the option of dribbling. Once again, defenders must be ready in basic position with the forward foot opposite the dominant hand of the offensive player. If that player is right-handed, defenders should have their left leg and arm forward to force the offensive player to pass or dribble with the weak hand. Have players defend with the palms of the lead hand up (see Figure 7.3), which will allow them to move easily, flick at, and steal the ball. This puts more pressure on ballhandlers and increases the chances of their committing errors leading to turnovers.

Figure 7.3 Live ball defense: lead hand palm up, trail hand palm facing.

Defenders play the ballhandler who has begun the dribble by cutting off the dribbler's path with the body and by maintaining ball-defender-basket position. The head should be in front of the dribbler with only the lead hand used to jab at the ball (when the dribbler goes to the defender's right, the left hand is used and vice versa) as shown in Figure 7.4. If the dribbler gets past the defender, the defender should run to recover or sprint to reestablish basic position and the ball-defender-basket relationship.

Caution players that they must maintain space between themselves and the dribbler when the dribbler uses a spin, reverse, or whirl move. They should prevent penetration first, then pressure the ballhandler in a ball-defender-basket basic position.

Guarding in a Dead Ball Situation

When a ballhandler has used the dribble, the two recommended techniques are (a) swarming

a   b   c

Figure 7.4 Defending to the right—point with left hand (a). Defending to the left—point with right hand (b). Ball flick—snake tongue (c).

the ball and attacking the player's senses while staying in a stance as shown in Figure 7.5 (pressure option) or (b) dropping back toward the basket while staying in the ball-defender-basket relationship to anticipate the next pass and help the team defense (sagging option). The latter can be used especially when the ballhandler is out of shooting range.

DEFENSE OFF THE BALL

This is the most challenging and crucial individual defensive skill that makes a significant

Figure 7.5 Attack the senses.

contribution to team defense. There is a natural tendency for players to relax away from the ball. However, they must overcome this and learn the importance of off-the-ball defense. Teach them that protecting the basket and supporting the defender playing on the ball are as important as attending to the assigned player away from the ball. These multiple tasks require greater attention than on-the-ball defense.

There are several other guidelines to teach players about defending away from the ball. The further the offensive player is from the ball, the further the defender should be from the assigned opponent, always maintaining a ball-defender-player position. The defender needs to keep a gap (a distance cushion to provide extra reaction time) as shown in Figure 7.6. In other words, the closer the ball is to the defender, the closer the defender should be to the assigned opponent away from the ball.

What the defender does before the offensive player gets the ball determines what the player can do with the ball. Defenders should keep the ball away from the assigned opponent in favorite spots on the floor. It is a good rule to always take away an opponent's strength on or off the ball.

Player cuts to the ball (ball-defender-player position) in the middle or power zone areas should be prevented. Teach defenders to

Figure 7.6 Open stance.

force offensive players to go around or away from a desired position. If contact must be made, the defender should beat the offensive player to a desired spot, make contact, and then reestablish a gap.

It will be easier to defend the ballhandler and support the defender playing on the ball if defenders see the ball at all times. Players should follow the ball visually to anticipate offensive cuts and careless passes.

Players away from the ball should assume an open stance, which allows them to see the

ball and their assigned opponent. In this position, one hand points at the ball and the other points at the opponent—a position termed *pointing your pistols.*

Several techniques may be taught to players learning to guard an offensive post player in or around the free throw lane. This situation may require either the ball-defender-player closed stance (hand across) (Figure 7.7a) or fronting stance (Figure 7.7b). As a general rule, the ball should be kept out of the power zone (post area).

Figure 7.7 Post defense. Closed stance—high side (a). Fronting stance (b).

When in a fronting stance, the defender should see the ball and stay in basic position without contact. This allows the defender to anticipate and move for the pass to the post. Offensive post players control defenders by establishing and maintaining contact. Post defenders should avoid contact unless they have an advantage in position; in other words, they should maintain a safe distance from the ballhandler and keep moving. This keeps the offensive post player (and passer) guessing.

The basic fundamentals also apply to defending a post player with the ball; defenders should stay in a basic stance with both hands ready. When an offensive post player does receive the ball in the low or medium post area, the defender should be taught to take a step back and reestablish a ball-defender-basket position. Maintaining distance will give the defender reaction time to defend against an offensive post move and also prevent the offensive post player from using contact to control the defender.

Defenders should use the help-and-decide defensive technique to combat the offensive tactic, which clears out one side of the court for the ballhandler to dribble-drive to beat the defender. The off-the-ball defender should be ready to help and decide if the defender on the ball is beaten or when his or her assigned player vacates the area.

SPECIAL DEFENSIVE SITUATIONS

In addition to the basic skills of defending on and off the ball, there are several other defensive tactics that can help your team defend against special offensive threats.

Screens

When an offensive player screens, or shields a defender to assist a teammate in getting an open shot, special tactics must be used. These include avoiding screens whenever possible—defenders should be in motion when offensive players approach them to set a screen. Screens can generally be defeated by (a) fighting through the screen, in which

case a teammate may help out the screened defender with a "show-and-go" move (Figure 7.8) or (b) switching assigned opponents, especially when a defender is unable to get through the screen (Figure 7.9). Notice that the defender guarding the screener switches "up," calls the switch, and contains the ballhandler.

COACHING POINTS FOR DEFENSE

General
- Get in a stance and stay in a stance.
- Use mind, body, and feet.
- Prevent easy scores.
- Keep pressure on the ball.
- Prevent penetration by pass or dribble.
- Move on every pass or dribble.
- Take away an opponent's strength.

On the Ball
- Maintain ball-defender-basket position.
- Guard players in a live ball situation; front foot to front foot, hands and feet active, and within touching distance.
- Guard the dribbler, keep head in front, jab with the lead hand, and run to recover when necessary.
- Guard a dead ball situation; swarm the ballhandler without fouling or sag away from the ballhandler.
- Jump to the ball when a pass is made.

Off the Ball
- Close out to the ball when it is passed to an assigned offensive player; sprint, break down, and prevent the drive.
- Maintain ball-defender-basket position.
- Get in an open (pistols) stance or a closed (hand across/thumbs down) stance.
- Keep space between yourself and the ball.
- play defense on offensive post players.
- Be able to help and make the decision to bluff or switch on screens, penetrations, or close outs.

Figure 7.8 Fighting through screens. Go over the top (a). Helper ''shows'' to help (b). Helper goes when teammate recovers or when offensive player leaves (c). Screen is broken (d).

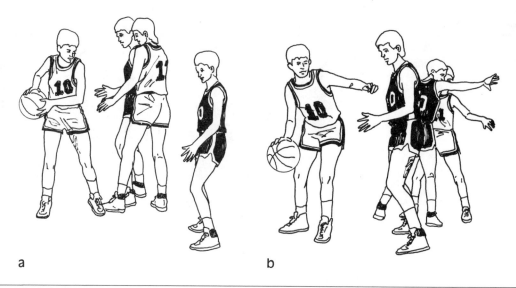

a   b

Figure 7.9 Switch the screen. Helper (on right; a) steps up to switch on player #10 (b). Helper calls the switch.

Traps

Coaches may also want to develop defensive techniques that can be used to handle an exceptional offensive player or function as a surprise tactic. Trapping occurs when two defenders double-team an offensive ballhandler (two-on-one). Emphasize that both players must stop the ballhandler from escaping the trap by being in good defensive basic position, keeping feet active, positioning themselves knee-to-knee, and keeping inside hands up to prevent a quick air pass. The objective is to force a lob or bounce pass and players should learn not to reach for the ball or commit a foul. All other teammates off the ball should close off the nearest passing lanes to prevent any passes from the trap into their zones. The best places to set traps are in the corners of the court.

Defensive Charge

The defensive charge—one of the fundamental defensive plays in basketball—is used when a defender has beaten an offensive cutter to a desired position on the floor and is in a legal guarding position. This defensive skill must be taught properly not only for its great potential as a team play (it can prevent an opponent's three-point play and result in two free throws for the defender), but also because it involves a contact skill that must be

developed progressively to avoid injury. The rules that apply to this situation are that (a) the defender is entitled to any spot on the floor that is taken in a legal guarding position, (b) the dribbler needs no room but the defender must be in a legal position before the offensive player's head and shoulders pass the defender's body, (c) away from the ball the offensive cutter must be given the chance to change direction (never more than two steps), (d) the defender must always be in a legal guarding position before a player leaves his or her feet to become airborne, and (e) the defender can move the feet backward slightly and can always protect the body.

Players should be taught these techniques for this play:

1. Get in and stay in a good defensive basic stance and keep feet active.
2. Take the blow in the chest area.
3. Resist giving up an established position.
4. Keep the arms out of the action and use them for protection.
5. Fall properly—with arms up and in front, the buttocks should hit the floor first, followed by the lower and upper back, and then the head in a curled position (see Figure 7.10).
6. Assume the officials will not call an offensive foul and scramble up to regain basic position.

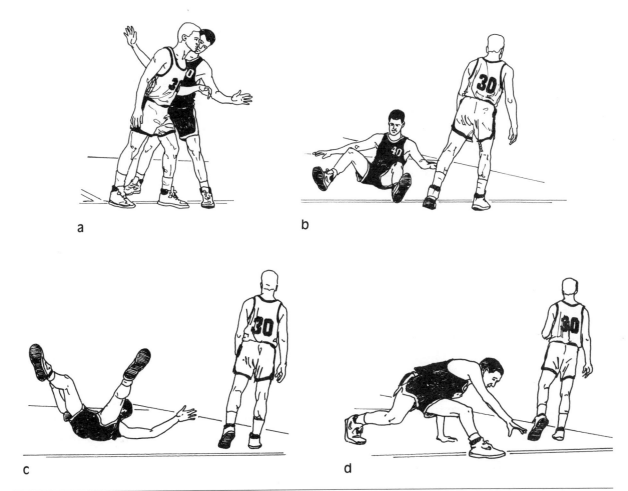

Figure 7.10 Defensive charge—falling properly. The defender must be knocked down (a). Landing—rear end first (b). Back roll, head curl (c). Scramble to regain basic position (d).

7. Know when to "take the charge." Disrupt the offensive player's movement but pick a situation where the player has poor body control and is not alert.

DEFENSE DRILLS

MOVING STANCE AND STEPS

Purpose: To develop individual defensive stance and steps.

Equipment: One ball for coach, half court (minimum).

Procedure: All players are spaced about the court, facing the coach with clear view. They assume a basic defensive stance at the coach's "palm down" signal and respond to coach's signals and commands with continuous defensive stance and step

moves. The coach uses the ball for most signals.

Signals/meaning	Movement
Palm down/live ball	Basic position; active feet
Ball in stomach/ back dribble	Slide forward
Ball in right front/ dribble drive right	Angle slide left
Ball in left front/ dribble drive left	Angle slide right
Finger point left-right/side dribble	Side slide
Ball in triple-threat position, then on the floor/off the ball	Closeout

Ball overhead/dead ball	Stay in stance/hands around ball
Shoot the ball in place/shot	Defenders call "shot," block out and rebound imaginary ball

LINE INDIVIDUAL DEFENSE

Purpose: To develop individual defensive skills in a progressive manner.

Equipment: Ball for every two players (at least four balls).

Procedure: Players form four lines on the baseline.

Offensive/defensive zigzag or zigzag in pairs. The first player in each line assumes a defensive stance with the next player in an offensive stance. The offensive player zigzags down the floor while the defender maintains defensive distance and a ball-defender-basket position. Players switch positions on the return trip.

CLOSEOUT

Purpose: To develop the individual defensive skill of closing out on an off-the-ball offensive player who has just received a pass.

Equipment: One ball and basket per group; ideally one ball and basket for every two players.

Procedure: When practicing closeout technique, the defensive player starts under the basket with a ball. The offensive player is in basic position facing the basket within a range of 15 to 18 feet. The defender passes the ball to the offensive player with a crisp air pass and closes out to defend. From that point, there is a live competition between offense and defense that ends when a basket is made or the defense gains possession of the ball. The dribbler is limited to two dribbles.

DEFENSIVE SLIDE

Purpose: To develop individual defensive steps.

Equipment: Full-court boundary lines.

Procedure: All players begin drill in court corner and use defensive steps as described. They follow the path noted in Figure 7.11. Players should allow the preceding player to reach the adjacent free throw line before starting. The drill should include the following 10 movements.

- Forward slide (1)
- Slide left (2)
- Closeout to baseline (3)
- Slide right (4)
- Angle slide-run-slide (5)
- Slide right (6)
- Closeout to the half-court line (7)
- Face belly to the sideline with an angle left side (8)
- Face belly to the sideline with an angle right side (9)
- Closeout to the free throw line (10)

Players repeat the circuit starting from the left side of court. They complete one circuit starting at each corner of one end line. It may be desirable to record the

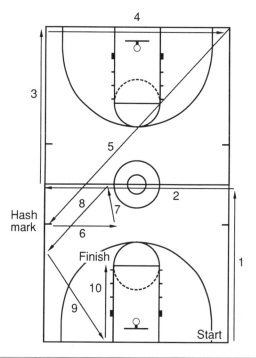

Figure 7.11 Moving stance and steps, may be started from right or left side.

time it takes to complete the circuit after using the drill several times.

THREE-ON-THREE, FOUR-ON-FOUR HALF COURT

Purpose: To develop individual defensive skills in a team setting.

Equipment: One ball, half court.

Procedure: Three (or four) offensive and three (or four) defensive players playing a half-court game centered around different offensive moves and situations to be played by the defender.

Chapter 8

Rebounding

In basketball, rebounding may be defined simply as gaining possession of the ball after a missed shot attempt. It is important for players to learn both offensive and defensive rebounding skills: The objective of offensive rebounding is to maintain possession of the ball and defensive rebounders attempt to gain possession of the ball. Rebounding is a major part of the game at all levels. In fact, it may even have a greater influence on a game played by younger players because of the higher percentage of missed shots at the beginning level.

REBOUNDING TOOLS

Rebounding, like playing defense and moving without the ball on offense, requires determination and discipline. Although height and jumping ability are advantages, the keys to rebounding are determination and technique. Statistics on the leading rebounders in professional and college basketball are not merely a list of the tallest players or the ones with the highest vertical jump. The same is true at the high school and grade school levels. Rebounding requires more than physical tools; considerable effort and proper execution of skills are necessary.

Without question, certain physical attributes are advantageous to rebounders. Players who are tall, have long arms, large hips, and well-developed leg and upper-body musculature are going to have an advantage over other players.

Vertical jumping ability is undoubtedly an asset for a rebounder. Coaches must see to it that all players learn rebounding skills, not just jumping skills. This does not mean that you should not encourage players to develop their jumping ability to its full potential. Use strength programs and other devices to enhance players' vertical jumps in your practices. But in addition to helping them jump their highest, you must also make sure they are jumping correctly. Proper jumping technique involves bending the knees, jumping off both feet, and using the thrust of the arms to reach full extension. Teaching players to jump in this manner will not only develop their leaping abilities to the maximum, but will also help them maintain their balance in jumping situations and will reduce the number of over-the-back fouls charged to them when rebounding.

MOTIVATING PLAYERS TO REBOUND

The first step in teaching rebounding is to convince players that it is a skill that is relevant and important for them to learn and perform in game situations. Explain that the entire team—not just those who are tallest, play post positions, or have exceptional jumping ability—must master rebounding skills. If you bypass this initial step, you will probably be disappointed by the rebounding performance of certain players during the season.

Reasons for Rebounding

Give players solid reasons why rebounding is a very important skill for all of them to develop. They must come to see rebounding in terms of its importance in getting and maintaining control of the ball and its key role in team offensive production.

Ball Possession

Rare is the player who does not like to shoot the basketball. Although it may sound simplistic, remind players that they can't shoot if they don't have the ball. Rebounding is the primary way of gaining or maintaining possession of the ball.

At the offensive end of the court, offensive rebounds to maintain possession frequently lead to quick and easy baskets.

Fast Break

The ability of a team to begin a fast break depends entirely on rebounding and turnovers by opponents. That is why teams with a well-developed fast break are also teams that have effective defensive rebounders. Whether your team offensive style is fast or slow, your basic strategy should emphasize getting the ball up the court quickly. This prevents opponents from sending their whole team to the basket for an offensive rebound on a shot attempt.

Players usually like to fast break, so it should be easy to motivate them to concentrate on rebounding. Put it to them in simple terms: No rebounds, no fast break.

Winning

Perhaps the strongest evidence of the importance of rebounding you can present to your players is the high correlation of successful rebounding with winning basketball games. One study examining rebounding and winning over a 10-year period found that teams that out-rebounded their opponents won 80% of the time. National leaders in team rebounding win more of their games than do teams that lead the nation in field goal and free throw accuracy. This statistic suggests that teams who gain possession of the ball only after their opponents score will at best trade basket for basket with them. The effective rebound allows a team to pull ahead.

Reinforcing the Motivation

It should be rather easy to convince players why they must rebound if they understand that rebounding is essential for ball possession and the fast break, and that it is very important to winning.

Praise and encourage players who give maximum effort in rebounding and single out individual players for particular rebounding accomplishments (e.g., most rebounds in a half, most defensive rebounds for the game, best blockout, etc.). Make sure they know how much their coach and fellow teammates value rebounding as a team skill and their efforts to perform well.

After making certain that all players feel responsible for rebounding and that they understand why they must rebound, explain and demonstrate the fundamental rebounding skills.

GENERAL REBOUNDING TECHNIQUE

The suggested rebounding technique requires that players gain inside position on an opponent, block out the opponent, and then get the rebound. Although rebounding seems to consist of three distinct phases, these occur as quickly as if they were a single action. The rebounding technique is commonly referred to as blocking out, and is sometimes called "boxing out" or "checking" an opponent.

All players should understand the following fundamental rebounding principles associated with blocking out. They are discussed individually in the sections following the list.

- See the shot.
- Assume the shot will be missed.
- Locate the opponent.
- Go to the opponent and block out.
- Go to the ball.
- Get and maintain possession of the ball.
- Move the ball out or down the court.

See the Shot

Players must be aware of when and where a shot is taken. Whether they are guarding an opponent on defense or attempting to get open on offense, they should know where the ball is at all times. Reemphasize to players the need to position themselves so they can see both their assigned player and the ball on defense and use their peripheral vision while moving to get open on offense. Players who are "blind" to the ball usually have other problems with fundamental skills such as positioning and movement that should be corrected.

Once they see a shot is being taken, players should call out "shot" to alert teammates who may have momentarily lost sight of the ball that they should get in position to rebound. Sometimes the shooter will call out "short" or "long" to give a teammate an edge on an opponent for position. The defender guarding the shooter has primary responsibility for making the defensive call. However, none of these verbal alarms are as effective as a player's own observation of the shot being released.

Assume the Shot Will Miss

Remind your players that every shot attempt means a potential rebound. Players must learn to always assume that every shot will be a miss and go to their rebound assignment.

Find the Opponent

Almost without exception, young players fall into the habit of watching the flight of the ball when shots are in the air. This can prevent them from being able to gain an advantage in rebounding position. Once the ball is in the air, their first reaction should be to locate the opponent they are responsible for blocking out or the opposing player nearest to them.

This does not mean that players should not be aware of the direction and distance of the shot, but they must avoid becoming spectators when the ball is in the air. Train players to be active rebounders by teaching them to locate an opponent while maintaining a sense of the direction and timing of the shot.

One way to find out if players are only watching the shot in flight is to use a simple rebounding drill. In this drill, the opposing player holds up a given number of fingers after the shot is released by another player. After rebounding the ball, the player guarding the digit-displaying player should be able to report the number of fingers the opponent held up. If not, the player was probably focusing too much on the ball in the air and not enough on the opponent.

Go to the Opponent and Block Out

Everything the player has done to this point has set the stage for the next step, the actual blocking out of the opponent. Your players may not have a difficult time with the first three steps, but blocking out an opponent is troublesome for almost all players and especially difficult for beginners.

The purpose of blocking out is to gain a positional advantage over an opponent for a rebound. Under normal circumstances a player is more likely to rebound a missed shot if positioned closer to the basket than the opponent. This is called inside position because the player is between the basket and the opponent.

Occasionally—when an opponent is far underneath the basket and a shot is taken from a long distance, for example—outside position (opponent between player and the basket) is preferable. Because this rarely happens, for our purposes in this chapter the inside position is the desired position for a player after blocking out an opponent. Figure 8.1 illustrates the difference between inside and outside position.

Figure 8.1 Inside and outside positions.

Before actually blocking out, a player must go to the opponent previously located, as in Figure 8.2. The player should move quickly and not allow the opponent to gain positional advantage. Teach players to use pivots and turns to help them gain inside position for the blockout.

Figure 8.2 Go to the offensive player to block out.

When blocking out an opponent, a player must be in a stance similar to basic position, with the following modifications. Feet should be parallel and shoulder-width apart, arms should be raised, upper arm parallel to floor, and bent at the elbows; and hands should be palms up. Figure 8.3 shows the standard blockout position.

Figure 8.3 Blockout—make contact with hands up.

The blockout is the phase of the rebounding sequence where players usually make contact with an opponent. Contact is normally initiated by the player with inside position. Because players must turn to the basket and be in basic position to rebound the ball (having already located the designated opponent after the shot was released), they will no longer be able to see the opponent being blocked out (see Figure 8.4). Players must use another sense, the sense of touch, to keep track of opponents' location. The buttocks and elbows are most often used for this purpose.

Figure 8.5 illustrates why it is so important that players make contact with the opponent. Notice in Figure 8.5a that no contact was made and as a result, the opponent has a clear lane to the basket and an advantage for the rebound. The player in Figure 8.5b, however, established contact and prevented the opponent from gaining inside position for the rebound.

Figure 8.4 Rear turn (right foot to right foot).

Despite widely held perceptions, basketball is a contact sport. Coaches must bear in mind that some players may be better prepared than others for the physical side of rebounding. In drills and games, match up your players according to size, strength, and readiness for contact.

Go to the Ball

The old saying that certain players have a "nose for the ball" may be true. Some rebounders just seem to be in the right place for a rebound on every missed shot. Part of their success may be due to some kind of rebounding instinct. More likely, however, is

that these apparently instinctive rebounders have studied where shots taken from various places on the court are likely to go when they are off the mark.

Help your players develop a rebounding instinct by pointing out the rebounding distribution diagrammed in Figure 8.6. Note that shots taken from the side of the court are much more likley (70%-75% of the time) to rebound to the opposite side. Players should learn to take a position on the opposite side of the basket from where the shot was taken (known as the weak-side or help-side position). On the other hand, they should be told that shots taken from the middle of the court more often tend to rebound to an area in the middle of the lane. Also, make sure players know that shots taken from close range will rebound closer to the basket than shots launched from long distances. Finally, players should be aware that some rims tend to make the ball rebound further away from the basket, whereas others seem to cushion the impact of shots and produce much shorter rebounds. Have players test the bounce of the rims during warm-up to find out whether they are likely to produce short or long rebounds.

Another explanation for the success of some players to get to the ball is hustle. Players who are good rebounders aren't lazy! They take the approach that every free ball is

a

b

Figure 8.5 Contact not made (a). Contact made (b).

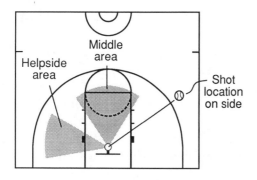

Figure 8.6 Rebound distribution areas.

theirs. These players are telling opponents, ''I want it more than you do.'' Inspire this mentality in your players by giving praise and other rewards for coming up with the most rebounds, loose balls, and steals.

Timing and jumping ability are two helpful attributes for rebounding. All the spring in the world means nothing if a player doesn't know when or how to use it. There are several useful drills for helping players get a feel for when they should leave the floor for a rebound. One especially effective drill is to simply have players repeatedly toss the ball off the backboard and attempt to grab the rebound at the maximum height of the jump for the ball each time. See ''Rebounding Drills'' for additional drill ideas.

Get and Keep the Ball

All too often a player will make a perfect rebounding play, only to lose possession because of poor ball protection. When teaching rebounding, emphasize to players that all their efforts to gain possession of the ball are for naught if they fail to protect it afterwards.

Figure 8.7 shows how a player should capture the rebound. Using this two-handed, strong, balanced technique for rebounding will reduce the chances of the ball slipping out of players' hands or of opponents dislodging it from their grip. Help players develop this skill by insisting that they go after every rebound in this manner. Remind young players to keep their eyes open and focused on the ball as they capture the rebound.

Occasionally the ball may come off the rim in an area where the player is unable to grasp it with both hands. In such cases players should attempt to either gain control using only one hand or to tap the ball to a teammate.

Maintaining possession of the rebound once it is captured is frequently more difficult than it might seem. Opposing players will try to knock the ball out of the rebounder's hands. Often they will trap the rebounder with two or even three players, making it nearly impossible for the player to pass or dribble the ball. It is very important that players learn to handle such situations.

When players rebound the ball in the vicinity of an opponent or opponents, their first move should be to bring the ball in under the chin with the elbows out and a hand (with

Figure 8.7 Capture the rebound. Always use two hands, two feet when possible.

fingers pointing up) on each side of the ball gripping it tightly (see Figure 8.8). This is called "chinning" the ball. Tell your players to chinit on rebounds and whenever handling the ball in a congested area. This allows them to capture and retain control of the ball. Tell players not to swing the elbows around to ward off an opponent, because this constitutes a violation or foul. Also tell players to keep the head up and look for teammates breaking downcourt or to an open spot in the backcourt.

Figure 8.9 Pivot away from pressure.

Figure 8.8 Chinit—elbows out, fingers up.

The most common situation facing a rebounder who gains possession of the ball after a missed shot is one in which a single opponent (usually one that the rebounder has blocked out) is nearby and attempts to steal the ball. Teach your players to pivot away from the opponent, as shown in Figure 8.9. Then the player should either have an open passing lane to a teammate, or be able to dribble without having the ball stolen. Caution your players not to put the ball on the floor immediately after rebounding a shot in traffic. This presents a very good opportunity for an opponent to steal or deflect the ball.

When rebounders find themselves surrounded by two or more opponents, the one thing they must remember is not to panic. If they are trained to remain calm, keep the ball in the protected position, and look over the entire court, options will present themselves. One escape move you can teach players is

the step-through technique shown in Figure 8.10. This technique can be used when the defenders trapping the player leave an opening large enough for the player to slither through. Sometimes an overhead pass fake will cause defenders to leave their feet and create an opening that the offensive player can step through. Players should not try to force their way through the defensive players, because this would probably result in a charging foul.

Figure 8.10 The step-through move.

Another option for a rebounder surrounded by opponents is to throw a pass over them. Even smaller players can use this approach if they make the proper fakes prior to the pass. Simple mathematics says that if the rebounder is being trapped by two or more opponents, then a teammate should be open or able to break open to receive a pass. Another strong possibility in this situation is that one of the defenders will reach in and foul the rebounder. Tell players to keep their composure when they are trapped by opponents after a rebound and wait for one of these options to open up.

Move the Ball

Once possession is assured, the player with the rebound must choose one of the available options. Whatever action the player takes should begin with the head up and the ball in a protected position.

Then, because the options facing offensive and defensive rebounders differ, post-rebound actions players will need to master vary accordingly.

OFFENSIVE REBOUNDING

Offensive rebounding is especially difficult if the defensive players are playing good ball-defender-basket defense because they will have the advantage for getting the inside position. However, offensive players can gain an edge by knowing when and where a shot is going to be taken. Emphasize the need for players to anticipate shots by teammates as well as to react to their own. Otherwise your players will have great difficulty being successful against good defensive rebounders. Trying to get around a rebounder in proper blocking out position is nearly impossible. Remind players not to go over the defensive rebounder's back when attempting to get an offensive rebound, because this also frequently results in their being charged with a foul.

Offensive rebounding is so important because it gives the offensive team another opportunity to score. This new life for the offensive team also serves to discourage the defensive players, who realize that they have lost a chance to gain possession of the basketball. There are many options available to the offensive rebounder.

Shooting After Rebounding

When a player makes an offensive rebound the first option is to shoot the ball. When your players get an offensive rebound they should first look to shoot, or if this is not possible to then pass to a teammate before finally exercising the option of dribbling. Emphasize that this is a very good time to take advantage of the defense. Because the defensive man was unable to prevent the offensive player from getting in position for the rebound, the defensive player may also be in poor position to defend against a shot. Among the types of shots an offensive rebounder can take are tips, shots without dribbling, and shots after dribbling.

Tips

If your players are well-skilled and big enough, they should tip the ball back at the basket. Tipping is actually a misleading term for a leaping player shooting a rebounded ball before returning to the floor. Tips that involve merely slapping at the ball with one hand are usually unsuccessful. Teach players to catch the ball and shoot it with both hands, if possible.

Tipping the ball is the most efficient way of taking advantage of the defensive players being out of position. By not bringing the ball down from the jump, offensive rebounders take away the defenders' chance to recover and give them almost no chance to block the tip attempt. Make sure your players are physically mature and skilled enough before suggesting the tip as their primary rebounding option.

Shots Without Dribbling

Encourage players to go up with the shot after a rebound without putting the ball on the floor. Dribbling takes time and allows the defense to recover. It also exposes the ball to the defense, making it more likely that a defender will steal or deflect the ball. If players have learned the correct rebounding jumping technique, they should land with the ball ready to go back up for the shot. They can shoot the ball from an overhead or chin it position but should always keep the ball up.

Often players simply develop the bad habit of dribbling the ball right after they get it, be it from a pass or a rebound. This is a habit that must be broken. Conversely, make a point of noting instances when players do not put the ball on the floor after rebounding, and praise them for this.

A good time to help players develop the habit of going back up with a shot after a rebound is during their individual shooting practices. Tell them that on every missed shot they should hustle for the rebound, get their balance, and, with shoulders square to the basket, go back up with another shot. They should continue to shoot and rebound until they make the basket, then start over from a new spot on the court. Soon shooting without dribbling will become an automatic response.

Shots After Dribbling

Although it should generally be avoided whenever possible, there are times when it is acceptable for a player who has grabbed an offensive rebound to dribble before shooting. One obvious example is when a player grabs a rebound far away from the basket and has an open lane to the goal. Because this situation presents an easy scoring opportunity tell your players to dribble the ball in for the lay-up when the path to the basket is clear.

Passing After Rebounding

Another option available to the player who has captured an offensive rebound is to pass the basketball to a teammate. The pass is the second option (after shooting) players should look for after getting an offensive rebound. Thus when they turn to the basket to look for the open shot after the rebound, they should also locate any open teammates to whom they could pass the ball for an easy shot. Once again, encourage your players to take advantage of the defensive players' having to recover after the rebound, by either taking a shot or passing to a teammate who has a good shot.

Sometimes an offensive team will choose to reset their offense, either to run a play or to take more time off the clock. In such cases, the option to shoot has the lowest priority for the offensive rebounder, and passing and dribbling become the more preferred options.

Dribbling After Rebounding

In most situations the offensive rebounder should dribble only if a shot or a pass are impossible. Dribbling usually only affords the defensive players an opportunity to recover and possibly steal the ball. And because the offensive rebounder is often surrounded by defenders, the chances of a turnover are even greater. With this in mind, continually advise players to look first for a shot, and then for a passing opportunity before dribbling when they get an offensive rebound.

DEFENSIVE REBOUNDING

Good defensive players will normally have a better chance to get inside position because of the ball-defender-basket position they maintain. Because of this positional advantage, and because of the need to limit offensive teams to only one possession each time up the court, there is great pressure on defensive rebounders to claim opponents' missed shots. The defensive rebounder must be adept at blocking out. The most effective way to establish inside position for the defensive rebound is to use front and rear turns. Have players practice these maneuvers alone at first, then against another player acting as an offensive rebounder, and finally against an offensive rebounder with actual shot attempts.

Turns and pivots are not always viable options for defensive rebounders. This is why it is important to emphasize that the key concern in defensive rebounding is not so much what technique is used to block out the opponent, but whether or not the opponent is effectively blocked out. Notice in Figure 8.11 how all of the defenders react to the shot by finding an offensive player and then going to the offensive player and blocking out. The defensive players form a weblike screen around the basket that the offensive players cannot penetrate. But if one defensive player fails to block out there will be a hole in the web and a chance for the offensive team to get the rebound. Blockout position and determination are keys to successful defensive rebounding.

Shooting the ball is not an option for defensive rebounders. However, there are various others available to defensive players making the transition to offense. The three principal ones are to hold, pass, or dribble the basketball.

Holding the Ball

Having the defensive player simply hold the ball after the rebound may seem pointless. But it is not nearly as questionable as having your players rush an ill-advised pass or force their way through opponents using the dribble and risk being called for charging. Unless your general strategy calls for players to fast-break no matter what, holding the ball tightly under the chin in chinit position after a defensive rebound is sometimes the most prudent move for a player to make.

If players hold the ball in the protective position under the chin following the rebound with knees bent and elbows out, opponents will have to foul them to steal the ball. Defensive rebounders should keep their poise and pivot away from the opponent while maintaining the protective position, and always immediately glance down the court to locate an open teammate. Then, if no player is breaking free, they should look for an open teammate in the backcourt to pass the ball to. Guards must remember to be available and open to receive the ball from a center or forward who is holding it after a

a

b

Figure 8.11 Before the shot (a). Shot is taken—go, bump, go (b).

rebound. These rebounders are usually less skilled ballhandlers, and they could very easily lose the ball to the opposing team if forced to resort to dribbling down the court.

Passing the Ball

The preferred method for moving the ball after a defensive rebound is the outlet pass. No opponent can outrun a sharp pass down the court. Emphasize that this pass is the first option players should look for after a defensive rebound, whether your game strategy calls for a fast break or simply moving the ball quickly.

There are several types of passes used to get the ball to a teammate breaking down the court. The long air pass (also called a baseball or one-handed pass) is used when a teammate is open at the other end of the court. The two-handed overhead pass is used when a teammate is around the midcourt area and there are opponents in the line of the pass. Finally, the two-hand chest pass is used to get the ball to a teammate who has broken open within 10 to 30 feet to the side or to the middle of the court. Because there is often less traffic on the sides of the court than the middle, teach players to first look for open teammates in this area on the rebound-side of the court before looking to the middle.

Passing is the responsibility of both the passer and the receiver. That is why it is so important that you teach players to get open after a teammate has claimed a defensive rebound. If the opportunity to beat an opponent down the court is available a player should take advantage of it. Guards should be instructed to move quickly to a spot where the rebounder can get the ball to them. A particularly good spot for guards to position themselves for outlet passes after a rebound is the rebound side of the court about even with the opponent's free throw line.

Good basketball teams take care to retain possession of the ball after defensive rebounds. Coaches must emphasize that the transition from defense to offense can either lead to a successful offensive possession or a return to defense, depending on how players handle the ball.

Dribbling the Ball

There are certain players who should not be put in the position of dribbling the ball from one end of the court to the other. In recent years, however, it has become more common for coaches to allow most players on their teams to take a rebounded ball the length of the court using the dribble. As bigger and bigger players develop both the ability to rebound and dribble, the benefits of the full-court maneuver have become apparent.

One major advantage of having a defensive rebounder dribble the ball to the other end of the court is simply that it eliminates the possibility of passing errors. There can be no errant pass if there is no pass! In addition, the rebounder/dribbler can quickly assume the middle position on the fast break without having to wait for a teammate to get open. Players must be able to respond to this situation. Have them practice spreading out and filling the passing lanes as they run down the court.

Another big plus in having your defensive rebounders dribble the ball is that it usually creates a numerical advantage over the opposition. Because one or more opponents are often slow to react in making the transition from offense to defense, a defensive rebounder/dribbler can get down the court ahead of them. If players are trained to recognize the situation quickly and hurry down the court, your team can frequently have a five-on-four or even five-on-three advantage.

REBOUNDING STATISTICS

Keep rebounding statistics for each player and for the team as a whole. Offensive and defensive rebounds should be recorded separately to help identify players having trouble rebounding at a particular end of the court. This information may make you aware of a problem with a player's offensive or defensive rebounding technique, or it might tell you that a player is not hustling enough at one end of the court. Individual rebounding statistics are one of the many pieces of information you should use in evaluating the contribution of each player, particularly those positioned nearest the basket.

COACHING POINTS FOR REBOUNDING

- Rebounding is the responsibility of all players on the team.
- Ball possession, the fast break, and winning are all closely associated with good rebounding.
- The best rebounding technique emphasizes blocking out the opposing player.
- The blocking-out technique includes the following:
  1. Being aware of when a shot is taken and assuming it will be a miss
  2. Finding, going to, and blocking out an opponent while paying attention to the direction and distance of the shot
  3. Going to and capturing the ball and getting it into the protected position under the chin
- Offensive rebounders should look to shoot, pass, and dribble—in that order.
- Defensive rebounders should either pass, dribble, or hold the ball, depending on their skills and the situation.

REBOUNDING DRILLS

REBOUND NUMBER

Purpose: To practice seeing the opponent and the ball when a shot is taken.

Equipment: Ball and basket.

Procedure: Divide players into pairs, with two or three pairs per basket. Put two players on offense and two on defense; one offensive-defensive pair on each side of the lane, halfway between the baseline and free throw line. Have a coach at each of the free throw lines with a ball. Defensive player on each side of the lane in basic position guards the offensive player. Offensive players

begin to move to get open. The coach can pass to them if they get free under the basket. Otherwise, the coach takes a shot and each offensive player immediately raises a hand and holds up a certain number of fingers. The defensive players try to block out the offensive players and get the rebound. If one of the defensive players gets the rebound and both defenders correctly name the number of fingers their offensive opponent held up, the offensive players move to play defense the next time.

LINE DEFENSIVE REBOUND ADDITION

Purpose: To teach players the techniques of defensive rebounding through simulation.

Equipment: Half court (minimum).

Procedure: The drill is organized in four lines on the baseline.

- The coach gives the verbal command "Defensive Boards"—The first player in each line sprints on the court 6 to 15 ft from the basket in defensive basic position. The coach designates ball location (left or right). On the command "Rebound," each player simulates the blockout, captures the rebound, chins the ball, and makes an outlet pass. Then the next four players sprint onto the floor in basic position.

Variation

- Boards in Pairs—The first four players sprint onto the floor in an offensive basic stance in triple-threat position (left or right) near the power zone and the next four assume a proper defensive basic position to pressure the ballhandler and support the defender playing on the ball. On the command "Shot," all four defenders carry out defensive rebound assignments, and all must make contact. No ball is needed for this drill.

REBOUND AND OUTLET DRILL

Purpose: To teach players the skill of taking

a defensive rebound off the backboard and making an outlet pass (or dribble).

Equipment: One ball per basket (the drill can be run simultaneously with two lines, one on each side of the basket).

Procedure: This is a defensive rebounding and passing drill. Have the receiver call the passer's name as he or she breaks to get open.

The first player X_1 passes to X_4, gets open for a return pass received with a quick stop in the free throw lane, and tosses the ball underhand above the rectangle level to simulate a defensive rebound (Figure 8.12).

X_1 angle jumps to the ball, captures the ball with two hands, brings the ball to the forehead, makes a front turn on the right pivot foot, makes an outlet pass to X_4, and takes the place of X_4. Player X_4 passes to X_2 and then goes to the back of the line.

The sequence is repeated on the other side with players X_2, X_5, and X_3.

THREE-ON-THREE CLOSEOUT AND BLOCKOUT DRILL

Purpose: To simulate team competition in a controlled three-on-three rebounding situation.

Equipment: Ball, basket, and half court.

Procedure: Three offensive players at 15 to 18 ft from the basket and three defensive players under the basket with a ball start the drill. The drill is played as a competitive "make it-take it" drill that is restarted only when a basket is made. In defensive rebound situations, the defense must clear the ball above the top of the key area before changing to offense. The coach may require the three defenders to stay on defense whenever an assignment is missed.

LINE DRILL—OFFENSIVE BOARDS WITHOUT THE BALL

Purpose: To teach players the offensive rebounding skills by simulation.

Equipment: Half court (minimum).

Procedure: The first four players make a "get-ahead-or-get-even" move from basic position, move to the free throw line area, jump quickly, simulate capturing the ball, land in the chinit position, and use a designated scoring move. They repeat this process at the half-court line, the opposite free throw line, and the opposite baseline. The return is made when all groups of four reach the end line. Offensive spacing (15-18 ft) should be kept with the player immediately ahead.

FIGURE EIGHT TIP DRILL

Purpose: To teach players to tip the rebound.

Equipment: One ball per basket.

Procedure: In groups of three players at a basket, the middle player starts the drill with a pass off the backboard (above the

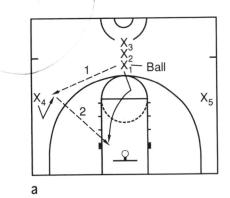
a

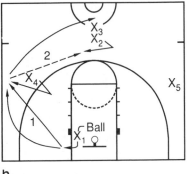
b

Figure 8.12 Rebound and outlet drill for defensive rebounding: start (a) and continuation (b).

rectangle) to the next player. The object is continuous, controlled tipping by the group for a given number of repetitions with players tipping and going behind (Figure 8.13).

GARBAGE

Purpose: To teach players to score on the offensive rebound.

Equipment: Two balls per basket.

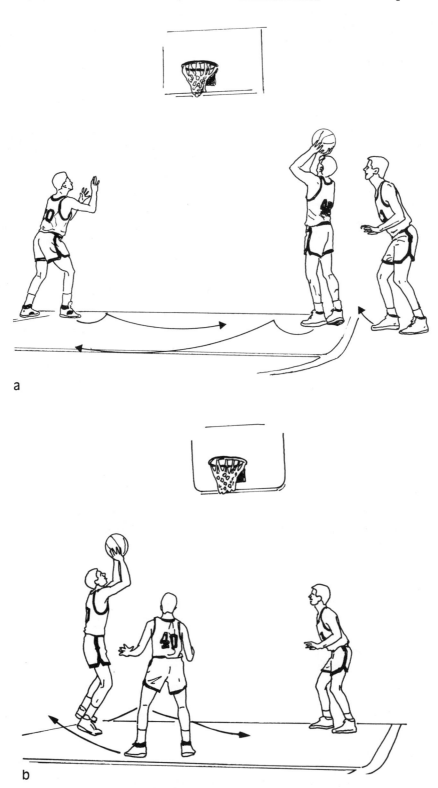

Figure 8.13 Figure eight tip drill: starting position (a); and tip and go behind tip catcher (b).

Procedure: Two lines of players at the free throw line area face the basket with a ball in each line. The first player passes the ball to the backboard with a two-hand underhand toss and rebounds the ball, then uses a designated scoring move. After scoring (and only after scoring) the player passes the ball to the next player in line and goes to the end of the opposite line.

NBA OR SURVIVAL REBOUNDING

Purpose: To teach players aggressiveness.

Equipment: One ball per basket.

Procedure: Groups of four to eight players at each basket with three players in the game at one time. If six to eight are used, extra players should be shooting free throws until they are rotated into the game. The coach or manager is positioned at each basket to shoot the ball (intentional missing) and act as a passing outlet for the rebounder. The rules of competition are as follows:

- Play starts with a missed shot.
- All three players attempt to get the rebound.
- The player who obtains the rebound is on offense, and the other two players become defenders.
- Rebounders use scoring moves; all shots must be taken in the free throw lane.
- The rebounder may outlet to the coach and get open for a return pass.
- There is no out-of-bounds boundary for play.
- Three scored baskets allows a player to rotate out (other players retain their totals).
- Significant fouls are the only fouls called. A player may lose a score by fouling or by not playing defense.

Part II

Teaching Team Tactics

Basketball is first and foremost a team game. Teamwork means reaching toward maximum individual and team potential. Your team will have the best chance of achieving this blending of individual play when your players have mastered basketball basics. It is important that all your players are able to play both offense and defense and perform all the basic skills. It will also be to your team's advantage if players are flexible enough to play any position.

To develop the best team play possible you will need to focus on two essential ingredients—playing hard and playing intelligently. This could be described as the two *Is* that each person must bring to the team—intensity and intelligence. Only the players themselves can bring their abilities to play hard and compete to coaches' efforts to develop their players' best possible individual and team performance. Coaches can't coach unless players play hard. If players bring intensity to the court, then both players and coaches can work to improve the level of intelligent play. Day by day, individual players and the team as a whole can develop their mental discipline and the habit of thinking through game situations. If both these things happen—players play hard and play smart—then they have a good chance of becoming a good basketball team.

To be a good team member, each of your players must learn that the team comes first and individual play second. Scoring is fairly easy in basketball—most players can create a scoring move alone. Players don't have to work with teammates to score, but they have a better chance for success when they do. Ultimately, one of the best measures of success will be the degree of teamwork shown by your team.

Chapter 9

Team Offense

Coaches should instill in players the confidence to go all out—to have fun, to learn and improve, and to take chances and make mistakes. This is especially true on offense. By preparing players to handle all situations, you will strengthen their confidence that they can be successful.

In order to prepare the team for all situations, the following areas should be covered: general offensive principles, responsibilities of players at each offensive position, offensive team tactics, and special situations for team offense.

GENERAL OFFENSIVE PRINCIPLES

Unless you are very familiar with the offensive strengths and weaknesses of team members, you should select a basic offense that can be adapted to a variety of players. It should be flexible enough to allow team members to use their individual strengths.

Any offense should have court balance, that is, it should produce high percentage shots with assigned offensive rebounders and assigned players for defense when a shot is taken. Balance also refers to mantaining proper court spacing—about 15 to 18 ft apart—between offensive teammates. Finally, offensive balance also consists of offensive rebounding and concern for defense when a shot

is taken. Making the quick transition from offense to defense (and vice versa) is called developing the transition game. Balanced scoring from players is always better than dependence on a scoring star.

A good offense includes player movement as well as ball movement. Scoring should come from the inside (close to the basket) as well as the outside (on the perimeter of the defense). This prevents the defense from concentrating on one area or one player. Remember that the execution of any system you design is much more important than the system itself. What your team does is not so critical as how well they do it.

RESPONSIBILITIES OF PLAYERS AT EACH OFFENSIVE POSITION

Each player on a basketball team has a position to play. It is related to role, ability, and skill. The three basic positions in basketball are guard, forward, and center (or post) (Figure 9.1). Some coaches use other names such as point, wing, and inside player.

The center is usually the tallest player, with forwards next and guards being the smallest. Centers and forwards tend to be the best rebounders, while guards are often the best ballhandlers. Guards also tend to play outside more than forwards and centers.

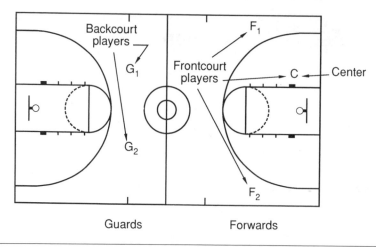

Figure 9.1 Player positions.

Guards

Guards are usually called the team's backcourt when grouped together. This grouping can be broken down further into point guards (normally the best ballhandler and often the player who directs the team on the floor) and shooting guards (also called "big" guards or "off" guards). Because of their dribbling ability point guards are often able to create a scoring chance for a teammate (such as the shooting guard) by penetrating and passing, that is, by driving past defenders to the basket and passing to an open or unguarded teammate. Point guards are called playmakers because they direct teammates and create scoring opportunities. The point guard will usually be among the best ballhandlers on your team, and should also be a leader who can be the coach on the floor. Choose shooting guards from among the best shooters and ballhandlers on your team. Confident shooting is another important characteristic to look for in a shooting guard.

Forwards

Forwards are sometimes called corner players because their normal offensive position is in the corner of the frontcourt. Most teams play a small forward and a big forward (sometimes called the power forward or strong forward). The small forward is more of a swing player who can play guard or for-ward and plays facing the basket where good ballhandling is a must. The big forward is often a strong rebounder and swings from outside to inside (back to the basket). Small forwards should be able to play as a combination guard-forward, handle the ball well, play outside on the perimeter, and rebound. Big forwards must be combination forward-centers.

Center

Choose players for the center position from among your biggest players who relish playing inside, near the basket, where contact and congestion are readily accepted. The center is usually the biggest player and plays inside around the free throw lane area in the high post (near the foul line) or in the low post (close to the basket) and outside the free throw or three-second lane with his or her back to the basket. The center and two forwards are collectively known as the frontcourt. (FRONTMEN)

OFFENSIVE TEAM TACTICS

Develop team tactics to prepare your team to face all basic defensive situations. You will need to include

- a fast break offense to keep the defense honest and put immediate pressure on the opponents,

- a press offense to be used against defensive presses, from half-court to full-court,
- a player-to-player set offense for situations where opponents guard your players individually, (MAN-MAN)
- a zone set offense to be used against zone or area defenses, and
- a delay or control offense to use when time and score dictate controlling the game and maintaining ball possession for longer periods of time before a shot.

Fast Break

One way the team can set up a good shot is to run the fast break where the team that gains ball possession brings the ball up the court before opponents can get into good defensive position. The fast break usually develops after a rebound, steal, or possibly after a made basket, and is the fastest way to make the transition from defense to offense. As soon as the defense gains control of the ball, they use the outlet pass or dribble to start the break—passing being the first option and dribbling the last when moving the ball up the court. Then, the other teammates attempt to beat the defenders up the court while staying spread out. Players should run at top speed under control when fast-breaking up the court. Remember to have one player stay a few steps behind the action in a defensive safety role for balance.

A typical fast break pattern is shown in Figure 9.2.

Press Offense

If the defense is defending on a full-court (all over the court) basis you will need a press offense to help your team get the ball inbounds safely. It is preferable to get the ball inbounds before the defense gets set. Designate a

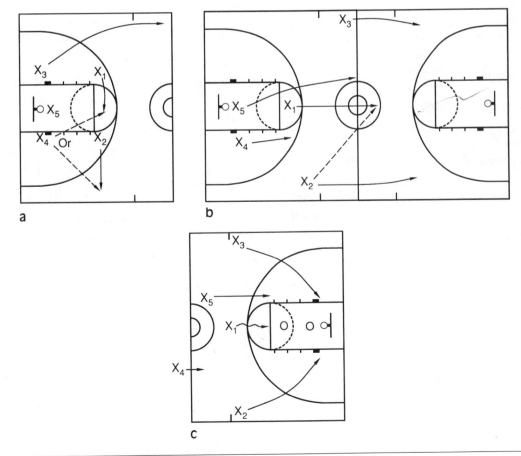

Figure 9.2 Fast breaks: starting (a), filling the lanes (b), and completion (c).

frontcourt player to take the ball out after all made baskets and quickly inbound the ball to a guard as shown in Figure 9.3.

Against any zone press teach players to attack the defense in the backcourt or front-court by having a sideline pass outlet, two middle pass outlets (short and long), and a safety-valve pass outlet (slightly behind the ball handler—O_2) as shown in Figure 9.4. Emphasize to your players the need to use good passing and catching fundamentals and remind them to move to get open, and keep their poise. Pressing defenses take chances. Players should be prepared to take advantage of those overcommitments.

Set Offense

If the defense is set and waiting, a set offense should be used to get a good shot. Your team should get into a basic starting formation and then use the fundamental skill moves with and without the ball to create scoring opportunities.

This basic set or formation may take a variety of starting positions. You should select a preferred starting formation that fits your personnel and favored tactics.

The 1-2-2 "Give-and-Go"

One offense for beginning players is the 1-2-2 give-and-go offense. It can be used effectively against player-to-player defenses. The give-and-go offense is a simple team offense that utilizes passing, catching, basic moves without the ball, and individual moves with

Figure 9.4 Beat the trap: form the three-player cup with a basket threat.

the ball. The 1-2-2 double low post or open post set is a one-guard, open post formation that allows any player to V-cut into the post area and keeps the middle open for individual offensive moves plus give-and-go options (Figure 9.5). The give-and-go offense from the 1-2-2 open post formation can also be used against zone or combination (zone and player-to-player) defenses by depending less on cutting and emphasizing more individual moves from stationary spots.

The rules for this offense are these:

1. The give-and-go from the point to wing pass is a pass and go-to-the-basket move after a V-cut is made by O_1. If the cutting player doesn't receive the return pass, then he or she should "balance the floor" opposite the first pass (Figure 9.6a). The give-and-go from the wing position to the corner position is seen in Figure 9.6b. Notice how floor balance is regained.

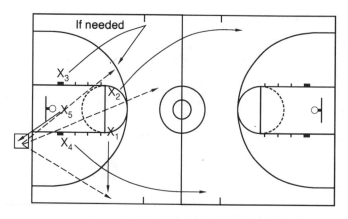

Figure 9.3 Press offense—get ball in quickly.

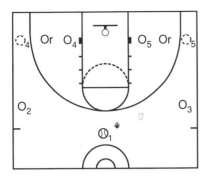

Figure 9.5 A 1-2-2 double low post set (may also be open post).

2. If a wing player is overplayed or denied the pass by a defender, your players should use a backdoor cut to the basket and replace on the same side (Figure 9.6c). If a corner player is overplayed, he or she should make a backdoor cut and come back to the same side (Figure 9.6d).

3. A wing or forward may V-cut into the post area (high or low). When players make ball cuts and don't receive the ball within 2 to 3 seconds, they should return to the same starting position (Figure 9.6e).

4. When a shot is taken the point guard (O_1) should go to defense near the half-court line and the other four players should go to offensive rebounding positions. This rule applies to all offensive situations: The offensive team should always have defensive balance and make a quick transition to defense. Coaches may prefer to have two players change to defense when a shot is taken.

The 1-4

The 1-4 double high post set is a formation that requires a good point guard. It is difficult to press; there are four possible entry passes; and the offense needs two inside players (Figure 9.7).

The 1-3-1

The 1-3-1 high-low post set has a point guard in front, positions forwards for individual

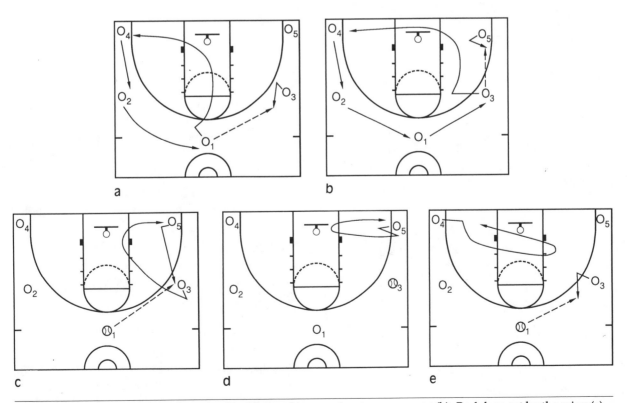

Figure 9.6 Give-and-go from the point (a). Give-and-go on wing-to-corner pass (b). Backdoor cut by the wing (c). Backdoor cut by the forward (d). V-cut to the post area (e).

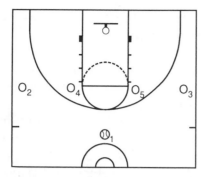

Figure 9.7 A 1-4 set or formation (point O_1, two wings O_2 and O_3, and two posts O_4 and O_5), sometimes called a double high post.

moves, and requires two inside players (the high post must be able to face the basket). See Figure 9.8.

The 1-2 Stack

Coaches might consider using a 1-2 stack formation. This set calls for a point guard in front, one open side for individual moves, and a stack on the other side. This may be used with one player (O_4) cutting to any position, while the other stack player acts as a screener and then takes up a single post position (O_5). The stack allows a variety of cuts by (O_4), as shown in Figure 9.9.

The 2-1-2 or 2-3 Set

The final possibility for an offensive formation is the traditional 2-1-2 or 2-3 set (Figure 9.10). This is a two-guard front with a single post (high or low). The side and corner of the court are open for forward moves. The 2-3 formation is more vulnerable to pressing defenses.

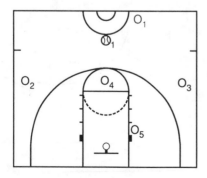

Figure 9.8 A 1-3-1 high-low post set.

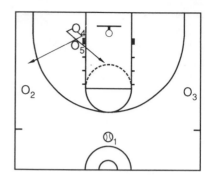

Figure 9.9 A stack set with a one-player front.

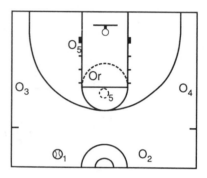

Figure 9.10 A 2-1-2 set (high or low post).

Zone Offense

Against a zone defense, coaches can opt for the modified, recommended, give-and-go offense or may select another formation. In any case, teach players to use the following rules:

- Perimeter players align in the gaps on the perimeter and step up into shooting range (Figure 9.11).

- Attack the defense, but be patient. Look for opportunities for dribble or pass penetration inside the zone.

- Watch floor spacing between other offensive players. This spreads the defense and makes it difficult to cover offensive players.

Coaches should also encourage player and ball movement. Because most zone defenses are ball oriented, ball fakes are also effective. This is a situation where a player should put the ball overhead in order for the defenders to see the ball and react to a fake.

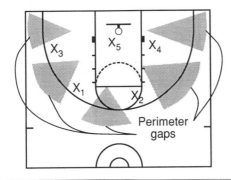

Figure 9.11 Zone offense—align in the gaps.

Control or Delay Offense

When the team has a lead late in the game, coaches may decide to have players spread out on the court and use the whole frontcourt to make the defense cover a larger area. This is called a delay game (or control game) and usually only close-to-the-basket shots are taken. When a shot-clock rule is in effect the delay-game shot rule is applied until 8 to 10 seconds remain, then the ballhandler looks for dribble penetration and other players start individual moves to set up a good shot. Time and score will dictate when the team should control the ball and use the clock (delay-game tactics). The most common formation for this offense is shown in Figure 9.12 where four offensive players are placed in the four corners and the best dribbler is out front in the middle of the court. Player O_1, usually your point guard or playmaker, constantly looks for chances to penetrate and pass. All offensive players should read and react to the defense, and wait for their defender to make an error they can capitalize on. Be sure to have

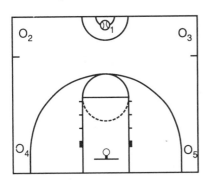

Figure 9.12 Four-corner offense—delay or control game.

good free throw shooters playing when using your control game because defenders may foul more, either out of frustration or by design.

SPECIAL SITUATIONS FOR TEAM OFFENSE

Team offense should be prepared to face a variety of special situations: out-of-bounds plays, free throws, jump balls, and last-second scoring plays.

Bringing the Ball Inbounds

Every team must have a plan for bringing the ball into play underneath its own basket and on the sidelines. Examples of formations and plays are shown in Figures 9.13 and 9.14, respectively. These can be used against any defense. Most important, your team needs to be able to inbound the ball safely against all defensive tactics.

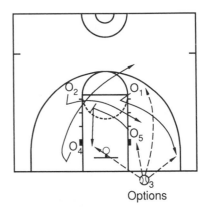

Figure 9.13 Under out-of-bounds play. O_5 and O_2 run a pick-and-roll screening play.

Free Throws

Free throw situations must also be planned carefully. On an offensive free throw, the two best rebounders should occupy the second lane spaces and attempt to gain an offensive rebound in the middle of the lane or to the baseline side of the defender. Player O_3 is stationed in a position to be alert for any long rebound or loose ball that might be tipped

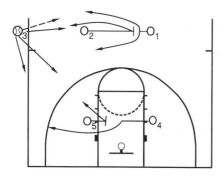

Figure 9.14 Side out-of-bounds play. O_2 screens for O_1, O_5 screens for O_4, and O_3 has four passing options.

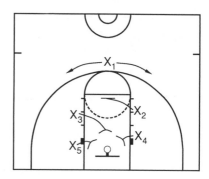

Figure 9.16 Defensive free throw. Four defenders block out or check their opponent on the free throw lane.

out, and O_1 and O_3 have safety responsibilities on defense and must not let any opponent get behind them for a long pass reception (Figure 9.15). For a defensive free throw situation player X_1 is the playmaker who must be alert for a loose ball or long rebound. Player X_2 blocks out or checks the shooter by getting between the shooter and the basket. Players X_4 and X_5 check the opponents on their side of the lane (second lane space) while player X_3 rebounds in the middle area (Figure 9.16). When a defensive rebound is captured all team members make the transition to the fast break.

Figure 9.15 Offensive free throw. O_2 is shooting, O_4 and O_5 occupy the second lane spaces on each side, O_3 is at top of circle (key), and O_1 is defensive safety.

Jump Balls

Special plays should be developed for jump ball situations. Taller players protect the basket in a jump ball near the basket. The smaller, quicker players defend the basket when the jump ball is near the opponent's

basket. No matter what the formation, the ball should be tipped to an open spot (where two teammates are next to each other without an opponent in between).

Last-Second Shots

The last-second shot situation, diagrammed in Figure 9.17, may be used in the delay game or in any situation where a move to the basket is made with 8 to 10 seconds remaining. This allows time for a good shot opportunity, a possible offensive rebound and second shot, but not enough time for the opponent to get a good shot at the other end of the court.

No matter what offensive situation, formation, play, or system is chosen, remember that execution is the key—it is not what players do but how well they do it that is important.

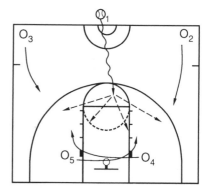

Figure 9.17 Last-second shot. O_4 and O_5 cross under basket (left hand touching left hand), O_1 looks to penetrate-and-pass, while O_2 and O_3 slide into scoring position ready to shoot. O_1 has four passing options.

COACHING POINTS FOR TEAM OFFENSE

- Be quick but don't hurry—Focus first on execution and timing, speed later.
- Maintain balance in all areas:
  1. Individual—Physical and emotional
  2. Offensive and defensive
  3. Offensive rebounding and defensive coverage (on all shot attempts)
  4. Floor spacing—Spread out and move the ball
  5. Inside and outside
  6. Passing and scoring
- Teach intelligent teamwork on offense.
- Teach players to put the team first.
- Encourage players to play fearlessly—To make mistakes but learn from them.
- Individual play should be developed within the team context.
- Ball and players should be in constant motion on offense and move with a purpose.
- Be patient with team offense. Play must be coordinated with player movements, so learning progress will be slower than with team defense.

TEAM OFFENSE DRILLS

SKELETON OFFENSE

Purpose: To teach basic team offensive formation movements and assignments.

Equipment: One ball, five players, and half court.

Procedure: Five players at a time take the court to practice team offensive formations, plays or movements, and individual assignments within the team offense. The offense should be initiated from all situations: backcourt, frontcourt, out-of-bounds, and free throws. Offensive play should be completed with a score each time.

This is a drill with five offensive players and no defenders.

FIVE-ON-FIVE TEAM OFFENSE-DEFENSE

Purpose: To teach team offense and defense in a progressive manner that culminates in five-on-five competition.

Equipment: Ball, basket, and half or full court.

Procedure: Five defenders and five offensive players practice team play. They should practice all offensive situations in order to prevent surprises on game day or night. The progression is to have defenders play dummy position defense, then no hands defense, before going to gamelike offense and defense with no restrictions.

Chapter 10

Team Defense

Build your team on a solid foundation. Defense is one of the most concrete and unchanging elements of the game. It can be the most consistent phase of team play and should be the heart of your team's strength. A team that prevents its opponents from getting good shots will be tough to beat.

In addition, because younger players have limited individual and team offensive skills, team defense can be an even more dominant aspect for beginners.

Convince players that defense is the key to building a foundation for team play. Beginners have trouble understanding the relation between defense and preventing opponents from scoring and winning games. You must convince them that defense and preventing a score by opponents is equally as important as scoring points for their own team.

Defense tends to be reactive rather than proactive—a defender will usually react to the moves of an offensive player. Players must learn to be aggressive and initiate action on defense—teach your players to act—not react—when playing defense. With determination and practice a team can develop good defensive play.

Remember, all team defenses are based on individual fundamental skills. Motivate players to develop pride in their ability to play defense. Any team can be made better by developing a sound team defense.

One of the basic precepts of team defense is to prepare players for action and prevent problems before they arise. For example, a player in basic stance can often anticipate moves by offensive players before they are made and then take that move away. Teach players to be ready for anything, which means being prepared to defend against opponents' best offensive moves. This makes the defender mentally and physically ready for any other secondary offensive moves by an opponent.

DEFENSIVE COURT LEVELS

There are many varieties and styles of defense, and these can be played at different levels of the court (Figure 10.1). Coaches can instruct players to begin defending the opposing team at any point on the court.

The full-court team defense is a pressing defense in which defenders guard or pick up opponents as soon as possible all over the court. In a three-quarter–court defense, defenders usually allow the first inbounds pass and then pick up offensive players near the free throw line or the top of the circle. The most common pickup point is at midcourt where the opponents are first guarded at the half-court line. Half-court team defense is the recommended level of defense for most

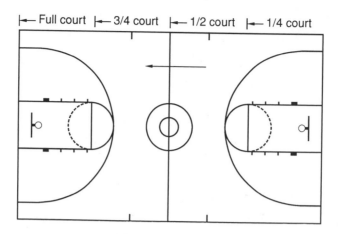

├── Full court ├── 3/4 court ├── 1/2 court ├── 1/4 court

Figure 10.1 Levels of defense—defending team protecting basket on the right.

teams through junior high school age. It is also possible to activate team defense at the top of the defensive key; this quarter-court defensive level is used if the other team has greater individual talent.

DEFENSIVE CATEGORIES

Team defenses fall into three general categories: player-to-player, in which each defender is assigned to a specific offensive player to guard or defend against; zone, in which each player is assigned a specific area of responsibility depending on the position of the ball and the offensive players; and player-to-player combination defenses having elements of both player-to-player and zone defenses.

Player-to-Player Defense

Emphasize the player-to-player defense as the basic defense that all players must master. There are several reasons why the player-to-player defensive approach is valuable. First, the techniques used can be applied in all defenses. For this reason, it should be the primary and probably the only defense used up through the junior high school level of play. If players in this age-group learn the basics of player-to-player defense, they will be able to adapt to any defense later. Second,

the player-to-player defense is the most challenging and also the most personally rewarding type of defense. No defender can hide in this type of defense: The offense is likely to score an easy basket after any defensive lapse. That is why player-to-player team defense promotes individual responsibility to the team. The basic principles of the defense are explained in chapter 7—Defense.

Zone Defense

Zone defenses assign each player defensive responsibility for a certain area or zone, rather than for an individual offensive player. Zone defenses usually change as the ball moves and are designed to protect a limited area of the court. They are often weaker in the gaps or seams between defenders and on the outside. They can be modified to disguise those weaknesses.

Zones can also be changed to lane defenses designed to intercept passes, trapping defenses (two players double-teaming one offensive player with the ball), or sagging defenses where the inside area near the basket is heavily protected.

The 2-3 Zone

The most commonly used zone defense is the 2-3 zone. Figure 10.2a shows the basic coverage areas and Figure 10.2b the weak areas of this defense. Use this defense when playing

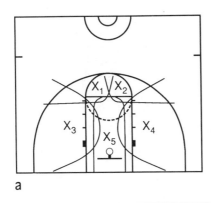 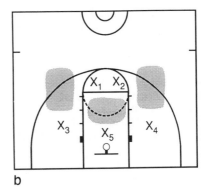

Figure 10.2 The 2-3 zone defense: coverage (a) and weakness areas (b).

a team with a good post player or when you need to ensure good corner coverage.

Figures 10.3a and b show the player shifts with the ball in different positions.

The 1-3-1 Zone

The 1-3-1 zone defense is also commonly used to cover the high post and wing area

well. It is strong in the center, wings, and point. The coverage and gaps are shown in Figures 10.4a and 10.4b. The shifts of the 1-3-1 zone are shown in Figures 10.5a and 10.5b with the ball in the corner and on the wing, respectively. Note that most zones revert to a 2-3 formation with the ball in the corner.

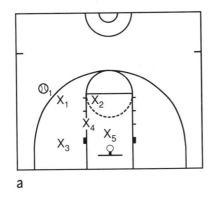 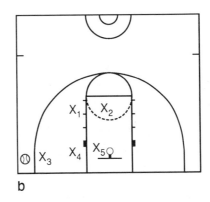

Figure 10.3 The 2-3 zone with ball on the wing (a) and with ball in the frontcourt corner (b).

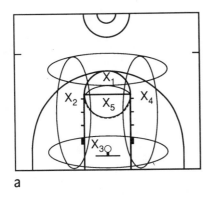 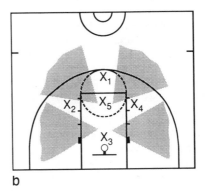

Figure 10.4 The 1-3-1 zone defense: coverage (a) and weakness areas (b).

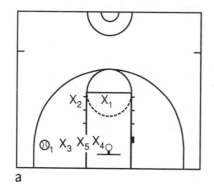 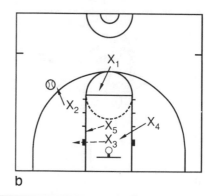

Figure 10.5 The 1-3-1 zone with ball in the corner (a) and with ball on the wing (b).

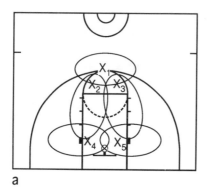 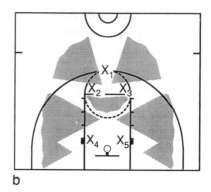

Figure 10.6 The 1-2-2 zone defense: coverage (a) and weakness areas (b).

The 1-2-2 Zone

The 1-2-2 zone defense has good coverage on the perimeter but is vulnerable inside. Its coverage and weakness areas are depicted in Figures 10.6 a and b. The movement and shifts of this 1-2-2 zone are similar to the 1-3-1 zone shown earlier.

Combination Defense

Combination defenses may take several forms.

Triangle-and-Two

Two defenders are assigned player-to-player on selected opponents while three defenders play a triangular zone as shown in Figure 10.7. To use this defense effectively coaches must decide on the extent of floor coverage and shifts for the triangle zone defenders and how they want the two player-to-player defenders to play (tight, loose, ball denial, etc.).

Box or Diamond-and-One

One defender is player-to-player while the other four play a zone defense near the basket. This works well against a team with one outstanding scorer or ballhandler. Two forms of this defense are shown in Figures 10.8a and 10.8b. Assign the opposing player who is the best scorer, ballhandler, or team leader

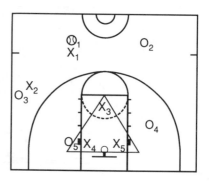

Figure 10.7 The triangle-and-two combination defense (X_1 and X_2 player-to-player).

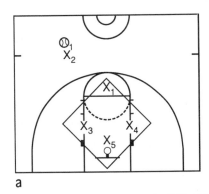 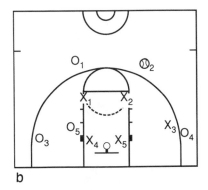

Figure 10.8 The diamond-and-one combination defense (a). The box-and-one combination defense (b).

COACHING POINTS
FOR TEAM DEFENSE

- Select one defense as the primary team defense. The player-to-player defense is recommended up through the high school level.
- Make attitude and motivation major concerns when developing team defensive play.
- Focus on practicing against all offenses. Prevent surprises for the defense during games by fully preparing your team for all situations in practice.
- There should be equal emphasis on offense and defense.

to the player-to-player defender. Determine who is the key player for the other team and how to take away that player's strength.

TEAM DEFENSE DRILLS

The individual defensive drills in chapter 7 can also be used to develop team defense.

Chapter 11

Bench Coaching

Bench coaching is the term used to describe coaching duties during games. The greater part of team preparation for games should take place during practice: Warm-up drills, game tactics, and cool-down exercises should all be perfected in practice. Coaches can give their teams a competitive edge, however, by developing the skills required for providing guidance and encouragement from the bench.

Coaches should first develop an overall game approach or basic concept of how they would prefer the game to be played. This might include a general philosophy plus offensive and defensive strategies or styles of play. The strategy must then be applied in developing game tactics—the overall game plan and the specific plans each player must follow in given situations.

Overall strategy should include a cooperative coaching approach. Define success in terms of potential, share decision-making responsibility with your players, involve all members of the team, and focus on player development, enjoyment, and winning, in that order. Coaches have the greatest influence on players and their development of a love for the game, and should take initiative in curbing the high dropout rate in athletics.

Games provide the opportunity to evaluate achievements and progress from both a coaching and playing standpoint. Approach games as a chance for coaches and players to have fun and reap satisfaction. Everyone should look forward to game competition, but point out the importance of a proper perspective on competition to your players. Focus on fun and development, asking them to only do their best to win. Tell them that winning is fine, but losing when you have done your best is OK. Each of your players should be able to find a degree of success in each game and this will help them develop confidence.

TACTICS AND STRATEGY

Long-range plans (strategy) and immediate plans (tactics) should be made to prepare the team for game competition.

Coaching philosophy, background, and coaching situation will dictate basic coaching strategy: style of play, offense, defense, and coaching style. Be sure to keep things simple and be yourself—develop a system that is best for you, your players, and your team.

You'll need to make some strategic decisions before games, during practice sessions. Game implementation, however, will require tactical adjustments and application. You should have plans for all game situations:

(a) Team offense (against all defenses)
- Player-to-player
- Zone
- Combination
- Pressing
- Special situations
- Individual skills

(b) Team defense
- Specific types
- Special situations
- Individual skills

(c) Player substitutions
(d) Timeouts
(e) Between periods (quarters, halftime)
(f) Postgame

Develop long- and short-range plans that prevent surprises for players at game time. Proper preparation pays dividends.

SCOUTING

The play and development of your team should always be your primary focus and concern. Opponents' tactics are of only secondary concern if you prepare your team properly and completely. However, knowledge of specific tactics of the opponents you play can allow you to better prepare your team and can also give them greater confidence in facing all game situations. Scouting, the careful observation of an opposing team during game competition, can give your team a competitive edge. Scouting a team means gathering key information on opponents' strengths and weaknesses that can be used in developing practice and game plans for your team. The three areas to focus on in scouting are individual players, team offense, and team defense.

To scout individual players, you should identify strengths and weaknesses of each player in terms of ability, offensive skills, and defensive skills. It is especially important to determine offensive strengths of opposing players so that your defensive tactics can be designed to take away opportunities for them to be used to advantage.

When scouting team offense, coaches should concentrate on these aspects:

- General style of play
- Press offense
- Fast break or transition game
- Set offense or patterns
- Rebounding
- Special situations (jump ball, out-of-bounds, free throw, and special scoring plays)

Defensive areas that should be scouted include the following:

- Type(s) of defense
- Level of defense (full-court, three-quarter, half-court, etc.)
- Amount and direction of pressure
- Help-side defense
- Rebounding
- Fast break defense
- Defense in special situations

A scouting form can make this task easier and help coaches use information more efficiently. It is best to have assistance when scouting—use an assistant coach, a student assistant, or an interested parent or fan.

At the high school level, it is also possible to use videotape for scouting purposes. Many schools agree to exchange videotapes for scouting purposes. You should not, however, videotape a game in which your team is not playing.

BEFORE THE GAME

To prepare a team for games, go over game strategy for the main areas needed to win. Use the information gained from scouting opponents to determine team defense and the opponent's anticipated team defense. Be sure to include individual defensive match-ups: Tell players who they'll be guarding and what individual strengths to expect from them. For example, you might say that an opposing player is a shooter, likes to drive, prefers a certain shot, or is very strong in some fundamental skill such as passing or rebounding. Next, decide on an effective offense against the opponent's anticipated defense. Be certain to mention team weaknesses as well. Select the offensive and defensive tactics you will use for this game in free throw, out-of-bounds, and jump ball situations. Finally, select two or three crucial areas—defense and defensive rebounding, for example—as keys to winning a particular game.

Game Warm-Up

A proper warm-up is needed for game preparation just as it was necessary for practice preparation. It should consist of physical warm-up (stretching and movement), warm-up work on basic skills, and mental preparation.

Since the team is preparing for vigorous activity, their pregame routine should include stretching exercises (usually in the dressing room) and moderate activity before the game. This prepares each player physically for competition.

Mental preparation should include a review of basic competition reminders and game tactics and plans. This might include (a) team offense and defense to be used, (b) opening tip or jump ball organization, (c) starting lineup and individual assignments, and (d) special game reminders about tactics or the opponents. This can be done in a short pregame meeting before going on the floor for warm-up.

Skill warm-up should include (a) shooting lay-ups and all other game shooting situations, (b) ballhandling, and (c) offensive-defensive half-court work (one-on-one, two-on-two, three-on-three, or four-on-four). The total warm-up time should be between 10 and 20 minutes and the activities should be carefully planned and executed. Using regular practice drills is an efficient, comfortable approach for players. For example, Ralph Miller of Oregon State University used his basic practice lay-up, split-the-post, and three-on-three half-court drills plus free shooting as a pregame warm-up for his team. It is recommended that any free shooting time (5 to 10 minutes) also be planned and

organized by putting players in groups of two or three (pairs are preferred). One player can shoot four or five shots while the partner stays away from the basket and acts as a passer-feeder. During free shooting, one pair of players should always be practicing free throw shooting (one shooter–one rebounder) until the shot is grooved. Have the free throw shooting pair switch off and find another pair to go to the line as they resume field goal shooting practice.

Lineup

A starting lineup must be selected and reported to the scorer well in advance of the start of the game. Coaches should select the five players that form the best starting group, not necessarily the five best individual players.

DURING THE GAME

This is the time when you have the greatest chance to carry out your coaching tactics on the sideline or bench. Coaches should be involved in the game at all times and maintain emotional control to ensure sound decision-making.

Defense

Make sure that your team defense is taking away opponents' primary strengths and that your team's defensive weaknesses are covered. If things aren't going well, make a change—substitute a player, change defensive assignments, or change your team defense. After deciding on the level of defense (half-, three-quarter–, or full-court) and the amount of pressure, you can change these at any point during the game. It is also necessary to make defensive plans for free-throw, out-of-bounds, and last-second situations.

Offense

On offense, coaches should have determined team offenses for player-to-player, zone, and combination defenses. When the opposing team uses a pressing defense, your team's press offense should be ready to go into action. An opportunity fast break should be prepared for situations where hustling the ball up the floor creates an advantage. Coaches should also make offensive plans for free throws, out-of-bounds plays, and last-second situations.

Substitutions

The pattern and timing of substitutions is another important part of bench coaching. Decide on a pattern to be used and adjust it to game developments. This can best be done by playing the less talented and less experienced players during the first half. Because players tend to have ups and downs, substitutions should be made to help them develop more consistency and allow your team to become more effective. Make sure substitution rotations keep experienced players on the court with inexperienced players. Inform players that substitutions will be made for a variety of reasons and that their purpose is to achieve the best team performance. Players must accept all substitutions and stay mentally involved in the game, whether playing or sitting on the bench. They should learn to be ready for any role assigned to them. Coaches can make this task easier for individual players by discussing their anticipated role in the team effort.

Substitutions should be made during the game according to defensive and offensive needs, fouls on individual players, and special game situations. In general, coaches should involve as many players as possible in the substitution pattern. All players who attend practices regularly and make a good effort should be given the chance to play in games. The ideal substitution rotation guarantees playing time for each player in each game, at least through the junior high school level.

Timeouts

Timeouts can be used for a variety of purposes, among them resting, making substitutions, and changing game momentum. When a timeout is called, coaches have only *one* minute during the timeout period to communicate their coaching points and instructions. This means players should hustle to the bench area. Have the players in the game sit in a group facing you with the remaining players standing behind them, also facing you. While players are organizing and getting water and towels, coaches should be analyzing the situation and organizing their thoughts. After this 15-second period, coaches have about 30 to 40 seconds to communicate their points and encourage players. Keep instructions brief and simple. In some situations a diagram may help explain the tactics you want to use. Always send players back on a positive note—be sure to tell them what to do and not simply what to avoid.

Halftime

During intermission or halftime you will usually have 15 minutes to prepare your team for the second half. This time should be broken down to include 5 minutes for organization and recovery and attending to individual players' needs, 2 minutes for review of the first half (good and bad), and 3 minutes to go over second half tactics (be sure to repeat any planned changes). This will allow 1 to 2 minutes for questions and 3 to 4 minutes for a second half warm-up. Be sure the warm-up is similar to the pregame routine and includes all important elements.

Near the End of the Game

The second half allows many more opportunities for bench coaching—substitution, timeouts, offensive tactics, and defensive tactics. Plan ahead and be prepared for the challenging pressure situations near the end of the game. Imagine what could happen and be ready for all eventualities. It will be necessary to prepare and rehearse tactics ahead of time. Coaches should also decide on the best personnel to use in a given situation.

Game Statistics

Coaches will find it helpful to have some factual statistics to assist them in a more objective evaluation of game performance on which to base future game decisions. Assign and train student statisticians to keep those statistics on the bench during the game so that they can then be used during the game, at halftime, and after the game to evaluate performances.

Keep individual statistics on field goals, free throws, rebounds, turnovers, assists, fouls, and recoveries for team players and the opposing players.

Efficiency ratings are a category of team statistics that prove most helpful in evaluating team offensive and defensive performance. These concepts were developed and popularized by an Ohio math teacher and coach, Paul Keller. A team's offensive efficiency rating (OER) is calculated by dividing the total points scored by your team by the number of possessions.

The standard for an excellent OER is 1.05, which indicates an average of 1.05 points scored for every possession. The team's OER is also the opponent's team DER. The defensive efficiency rating (DER) for your team is calculated by dividing the number of points allowed by the number of opponents' ball possessions.

An excellent DER is .85 points per possession. If the OER and DER possession statistics are kept in groups of 10 possessions it is easy to estimate the average. For example, if a team scores 11 points during its first 10 possessions (OER = 1.10) and allows 8 points during those 10 possessions (DER = .80), these values can be easily calculated.

POSTGAME EVALUATIONS

Coaches should evaluate individual and team performance after each game in order to determine status, progress, and adjustments in practice plans. Use all game statistics and videotapes, as well as your subjective evaluation of the game. In addition, give your players performance feedback in order to speed their development.

Individual and team performance can also be evaluated with the use of prepared checklists. These tools can be used for both practice and game evaluations. Use the checklists after each game and periodically for practice.

Index

Passes. *See also* Ballhandling, passing and catching
   baseball, 21-22
   bounce, 21
   chest, 20-21
   overhead, 21, 22
   push, 22, 23
Perimeter, playing. *See* Outside moves
Perimeter drills, 53-55
Permanent pivot foot moves
   crossover step, 49-50, 51
   direct drive, 48
   hesitation or step-step, 48-49, 50
   rocker step, 49, 50
Pivots. *See* Steps (pivots)
Players, individual
   contribution to team efforts by, 1
   positions for, 95-96
Pointing your pistols position, 69
Post, playing. *See* Inside moves
Post progression drill, 63

R
Rebound and outlet drill, 88-89
Rebounding
   coaching points for, 88
   defensive
      description of, 85-86
      dribbling the ball during, 87
      holding the ball during, 86-87
      passing the ball during, 87
   description of, 77
   drills for, 88-91
   motivating players for, 77-78
   offensive
      description of, 84
      dribbling after rebounding, 85
      passing after rebounding, 85
      shooting after rebounding, 84-85
   and pivoting, 7
   reasons for
      ball possession, 78
      fast break, 78
      winning, 78
   statistics for, 87-88
   technique for, 78-84
   tools for, 77
Rebounding drills, 88-91
Rebounding technique
   assuming the shot will miss, 79
   blocking out the opponent, 79-81
   description of, 78-79
   finding the opponent, 79
   getting and keeping the ball, 82-84
   going to the ball, 81-82
   moving the ball, 84
   seeing the shot, 79
Rebound number drill, 88

S
Scouting, 112

Screen moves
   setting, 15-16
   types of, 15
   using, 16
Set and jump shot techniques
   balance, 36
   description of, 35
   elbow, 36, 37
   follow-through, 37
   grip, 36
   release, 36-37
   target, 36
   three-point shot, 37-38
   wrist, 36
Shooting
   drills for, 41-45
   field goal
      coaching points for, 38
      description of, 33-34
      desired percentages for, 33
      drills for, 41-42
      lay-ups, 34, 35
      post hook-shot principles, 38, 39
      set and jump shot techniques, 35-38
   free throw
      coaching points for, 41
      and confidence, 39-40
      description of, 38-39
      drills for, 44-45
      techniques for, 40-41
   general
      coaching points for, 33
      description of, 33
Shooting drills, 41-45
Shot moves, 15
Skeleton offense drill, 103
Spin pass outside moves drill, 54
Spin pass post moves drill, 63
Stance check drill, 9
Stance mirror drill, 9
Starting lineup, 113
Starts
   coaching points for, 6
   description of, 5
   drills for, 9-11
   front foot first, 5
   point-push-pull, 5-6
Statistics
   during a game, 114-115
   for rebounding, 87-88
Steps (pivots)
   coaching points for, 7
   description of, 5, 6-7
   drills for, 9-11
Stops
   coaching points for, 8
   description of, 5, 7
   drills for, 9-11
   quick, 7-8
   stride, 8

About the Author

Jerry Krause has been coaching the basics of basketball since 1959. His experience at the elementary, high school, college, and Olympic levels uniquely qualifies him to write a book that helps to improve the skills of players at all levels of play.

Jerry is a professor of physical education at Eastern Washington University and assistant basketball coach at Gonzaga University in Spokane, Washington. He received the 1988 State Honor Award from the Washington Alliance for Health, Physical Education, Rec-reation and Dance for outstanding teaching and coaching in college physical education. Jerry, as a member of the National Associa-tion of Basketball Coaches, is the chair of their National Research Committee and wrote the 1986 Code of Ethics. He is also a member and past president of the National Association of Intercollegiate Athletics Basketball Coaches Association.

Jerry is the author of two other Leisure Press books, *The Basketball Bible* and the *Basketball Resource Guide*.